brilliant

body language

brilliant

body language

Impress, persuade and succeed with the power of body language

Max A. Eggert O.P.C.

Prentice Hall
is an imprint of

Harlow, England • London • New York • Boston • San Francisco • Toronto • Sydney • Singapore • Hong Kong
Tokyo • Seoul • Taipei • New Delhi • Cape Town • Madrid • Mexico City • Amsterdam • Munich • Paris • Milan

PEARSON EDUCATION LIMITED

Edinburgh Gate
Harlow CM20 2JE
Tel: +44 (0)1279 623623
Fax: +44 (0)1279 431059
Website: www.pearsoned.co.uk

First published in Great Britain in 2010

ISBN: 978-0-273-74074-2

British Library Cataloguing-in-Publication Data
A catalogue record for this book is available from the British Library

Library of Congress Cataloging-in-Publication Data
Eggert, Max.
  Body language : impress, persuade and succeed with the power of body
language / Max Eggert.
     p. cm.
  Includes bibliographical references and index.
  ISBN 978-0-273-74074-2 (pbk. : alk. paper) 1. Body language. I. Title.
  BF637.N66E44 2010
  153.6'9--dc22
                              2010033907

10 9 8 7 6 5 4 3 2 1
14 13 12 11 10

Illustrations by Sarah Arnold
Typeset in 10/14pt Plantin by 3
Printed in Great Britain by Henry Ling Ltd, at the Dorset Press, Dorchester, Dorset

This work is dedicated to Joan Elizabeth Eastwood who, no matter how I try and in spite of my very best endeavours, reads me like a book and still forgives and loves me.

Contents

About the author

'*Max is an international management psychologist who has the gift of making the complexities of human behaviour understandable and relevant to business.*'

Financial Times

Max A. Eggert is Chief Psychologist with Transcareer, an International Management Psychology Consultancy. He has been interviewed frequently on TV, radio and in the print media both in Europe and Australia. His work and publications have been reviewed both in the professional journals and the specialist media. He has also lectured at premier universities as well as many leading professional conferences.

Max first read theology as a preparation for the priesthood, then through his interest in people undertook degrees in psychology and industrial relations. Several of his books are on the recommended reading lists of London, Sydney, Harvard, Westminster and Sussex Universities.

Married to Jane with four children between them, Max and his family live in Bondi Beach, Australia and, as an Anglo-Catholic priest, Max's joy and privilege is being on the pastoral team of St Mark's Granville in the Archdiocese of Sydney. When not writing, consulting or counselling, his other consuming passions are riding his thoroughbred, Zeus, walking his dogs, Daisy and Bana, attempting to stop the three cats, Solomon, Sheba and Pierre, from destroying china mementoes and failing to stop Mary, his Eclectus parrot, from using expletives.

Max can be contacted at Max@transcareer.com.au and you can discover more about his work at www.transcareer.com.au

Acknowledgements

First, to my beautiful wife Jane-Lizbeth, who put up with my absence by banishing me to the study, and driving a hard bargain that no Chardonnay could touch my lips until the day's quota of 1,500 words – at least – had been written.

Secondly, this work would not have been possible but for the trust, support and encouragement of the London Pearson publishing team providing guidance 12,000 miles away from my home in Bondi Beach. The stars pulling this project together have been Rachel Hayter, who hounded me to make the deadline; Emma Devlin, for sorting out the legals and coordinating the artwork; Helena Caldon, who coped so well with my dyslexia by correcting my creative spelling; Sarah Arnold, who captured my continually changing and picky demands on the nuances of the artwork; with the whole team, including me, kept on track, committed and motivated by Samantha Jackson, all under the watchful eye of Richard Stagg.

Thanks also to the team at Transcareer in Sydney for assisting with considerable academic research and, as always, keeping me humble.

Benedicam Dominum qui tribuit mihi intellectum: insuper et usque ad noctem increpuerunt me renes mei.

Publisher's acknowledgements

We are grateful to the following for permission to reproduce copyright material:

The tips for work text on page 46–7 from *The Perfect Interview*, published by Random House Business Books. Reprinted by permission of The Random House Group Ltd; The 75 body-language signs table on page 187–91 courtesy of Gabrielle Griffin.

In some instances we have been unable to trace the owners of copyright material, and we would appreciate any information that would enable us to do so.

Academic references

Academic references are given for three main reasons:

1 Some of us are naturally sceptical about this subject – if
   someone puts their hands behind their head or if they point
   their feet in a certain direction then one might justifiably
   come to the conclusion that an individual is just more
   comfortable sitting that way. But these actions might
   also have a more significant meaning, and the academic
   references outline research that provides repeatable
   evidence that such actions may indicate more that just an
   individual's preference or comfort.

2 A book such as this is really an introduction to the subject
   of body language, and so it is rather like a stone bouncing
   on the top of the water of this important topic. However,
   there is much that lies below the surface and some readers
   will want to know more, which can be found by pursuing
   the references.

3 Finally, I would hate anyone to think that I knew all this
   information; like any psychologist, I stand on the shoulders
   of giants.[1]

Reference

[1] Sir Isaac Newton's incisive truism in a letter to Robert Hooke (1676).

Introduction

How it all started

Occasionally he verbalises! Even before you uttered a word you could communicate. Every mother knows her baby's different cries – the cry for hunger, the cry of discomfort, the cry of pain and the cry for not getting your own way. Even before you understood a word you understood a smile, a frown and perhaps even a look of anxiety.

Our first language

As primates we were communicating to each other long before there were words. This was a sophisticated language, too – how else could you bring down a mammoth 30 times heavier and perhaps 30 times more powerful than yourself, along with other members of your family/tribe, armed with just long sticks with a stone strapped at one end?

It was Darwin[1] who was one of the first to notice that emotional signs in animals were also mirrored by humans. Joy, fear and pain in apes, in terms of facial characteristics, very similar to ours. It then became a small step to go from that observation to the study of body language in humans.

Even complex messages can be sent and interpreted without a word being spoken. In the armed services there is as minor infringement called 'dumb insubordination'. You have not said a word and yet because of your body language – both meant by you and interpreted correctly by your superior – you are put on a charge.

Body language is the condiment on the table of words

Just imagine how boring theatre would be if the actors just stood on the stage and delivered their lines in a monotone and monologue. Even with great playwrights, what makes their work come to life is the body language of the actors and the way their words are delivered. Actors not only use their bodies to show emotion but also employ small subtle movements – usually their hands as commas and full stops – as they deliver their lines. For emphasis, whole body movements act like a new paragraph, indicating to the audience that a new mood or an important nuance is to be noted.

Mime takes this to the extreme, so that even small children have little difficulty in understanding sometimes quite complicated storylines and humour. In fact, this ability is good news for us, because if actors can learn to use body language to match their characters and the thrust of the drama, then so, with observation and practice, can we.

Inevitably, as you cover the various sections in this book you will discover some duplication. The concept of smiling or the word smile occurs over 80 times in the following pages. Less frequent are the concepts of eye contact or standing tall, but they too are given good coverage. Such body language actions are the building blocks of many aspects of human interaction. Rather like cooking utensils in the hands of a master chef, these movements can be used to create many varying dishes according to different interpersonal circumstances. Where appropriate, the more common concepts are detailed in a major section. Where such items are duplicated in other chapters, the appropriate cross-referencing is given.

Reference

[1] Darwin, C. (1872), *The Expressions of Emotions in Man and Animals.*

CHAPTER 1

Our other language – an introduction

What is body language?

Body language is just what it says – how we communicate with others using all the parts of our body: the total of all the movements we make whilst talking, listening and even when we are thinking. Literally, from head to toe we are continually sending out messages and we do it unconsciously!

What is and what is not body language

Body language is part of non-verbal communication (NVC). We can also make a statement to others by the clothes we choose to wear, how we wear them, how we greet others, how we walk and even how we eat. Nor does it stop there, for we also communicate to others not just with the words we use but also how we have selected those specific words from our vocabulary, the way we say them and how we string them together.

Signs that we make with our hands and fingers that have a specific word or phrase counterpart – for example, thumbs up for 'OK', thumb and first finger together meaning 'perfect' or 'really good',[1] finger across the throat for 'cut', 'stop' or 'kill' – are all learnt and even have different meanings in different cultures. Such signs are deliberate and are made consciously, so they are not body language in the true sense and we will not be covering them.

Why is body language so powerful?

It could be strongly argued that as humans we have been communicating through body language and signs far longer than we have been using formal language with vocabulary and grammatical rules. This formal language developed by mirroring the growth of our cognitive abilities.

Some linguistic neuropsychologists have argued that as humans our brains may be hard-wired to communicate and understand the nuances of our unconscious body language. Ekman,[2] in his seminal work on facial signs, found that there were six basic emotional faces (anger, disgust, fear, happiness, sadness, surprise) which are understood all over the globe, from the most primitive of cultures to the most advanced.

Even small children show emotion at a very young age. The baby on the left is gaining as much pleasure from sucking his thumb as the young child on the right is showing fear. Both pictures confirm that our six emotional faces, many of which we share with our fellow primates, are probably hard-wired into our brains.

Body language (noun)

Non-verbal, mostly unconscious communication made by an individual through facial expressions, gestures, movements and postures.

What body language does

Body language is the catalyst between the words we say to each other so that the full meaning, nuance and implication can blossom. If what we are saying with our bodies can be understood intuitively by another and we in turn understand their body language, then we have a very powerful tool box to employ in our relationship with others. We will be able to comprehend and understand whether someone is telling the truth, if they like us or not and how they feel about a topic or situation. For example, the full meaning of the words 'they are eating apples' or 'the killing of the hunters was horrible'[3] does not come from the words alone but is immediately comprehensible from body language and NVC.

Which of the six basic emotions is being expressed here? Can you find seven items to support your conclusion? Answers on page 221.

Occasionally, understanding body language can also assist in assessing how someone is going to respond to a situation and to predict what they might do next.

▶ brilliant example

Body language can also act as a catalyst in many a social interaction. Every good host knows that when a dinner guest politely says 'No' when refusing an offer of another slice of pavlova, that they should offer it again because the body language indicates that they are really desperate for another slice, irrespective of the cholesterol consequences, but are feeling bound by etiquette.

Why is body language important?

Over 40 years ago Professor Mehrabian,[4] who was an engineer before he became interested in psychology, suggested that in certain face-to-face communications – especially when someone is trying to interpret attitudes – there are three major components:

- what is said;
- how it is said;
- the facial expressions.

The most fascinating outcome of this research into attempting to understand someone, especially in interpreting the feelings and attitude of the other person, was that if their body language did not match what they were saying (psychologists call this incongruency) it was the body language that was the deciding factor. This result was not what the researchers were expecting.

Figure 1.1 gives an indication of the influence of the three main channels of communication.

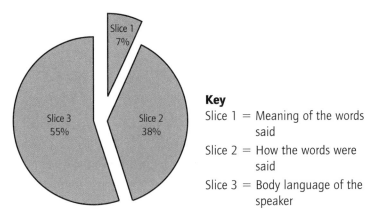

Key
Slice 1 = Meaning of the words said
Slice 2 = How the words were said
Slice 3 = Body language of the speaker

Figure 1.1 Three main channels of communication.

It is important to note that there have been many subsequent studies of Mehrabian's work calling into question these percentages, such as that by Argyle. Nevertheless, whilst psychologists can argue over the percentages of the ratios, the significance of body language in the context of understanding and comprehension must still be recognised and acknowledged.

So the words employed might be what the other person would like you to understand, but how they are delivered will convey the real meaning of the speaker.[5]

brilliant impact

Here are just a few areas where this work on body language becomes significant for almost every aspect of our social world:

- If we wish to be understood and our communications to be clear, whether in family, social or work situations.
- If we wish to really understand someone else and know how they like to express themselves.
- If we wish to convince or persuade someone to our point of view, whether it be a friend, whilst managing others, at an interview, in a sales opportunity or during a negotiation.

▶

- If we wish to know whether or not we are being told the truth by another person or even when someone is putting their own spin on a situation.

- If we wish to be able to recognise the emotions behind the words so that we can be empathetic if that person is in pain, or be prepared should they wish to take advantage of us.

- If we wish to predict accurately what someone might do next.

In summary then, body language and non-verbal communication are essential for understanding others, their true feelings and emotions, their views and their actions.

Body language and personal success

Conversely, in much the same way we need to be aware of our own body language if we are to be more effective.

> *'No man is an island, entire of itself;*
> *every man is a piece of the continent,*
> *a part of the main.'*

So wrote John Donne in his seventeenth meditation, and we know it to be true. Each one of us lives and breathes in community with others, with communication being the conduit between us. However, if we are to succeed we must be able to relate effectively. The more we understand about our own body language and what we are 'saying' in our non-verbal communication, the more likely we are to achieve success.

Organisations invest thousands of pounds each year training their sales staff in the craft of understanding the body language of others and controlling their own. Such monies would not be spent if there was not a significant return on the investment.

'The most important thing in communication is to hear what isn't being said.'

Peter Drucker, management consultant

brilliant recap

- We all speak body language fluently.
- Body language gives full meaning to what we say.
- Body language can indicate what someone is going to do next.
- Body language is essential for understanding others.
- Understanding body language is essential for successful relations with others.

References

[1] Morris, D. (1977), *Manwatching*.

[2] Ekman, P. (1982), *Emotion in the Human Face*, 2nd edition.

[3] There are also grammatical rules that assist in comprehension; these two examples come from N. Chomsky's work on transformational grammar (1956), 'Three models for the description of language', *IRE Transactions on Information Theory* 2: 113–124, and his extensive work following that groundbreaking paper.

[4] Mehrabian, A. (1971), *Silent Messages*.

[5] Argyle, M., Salter, V., Nicholson, H., Williams, M. and Burgess, P., (1970), 'The communication of inferior and superior attitudes by verbal and non-verbal signals', *British Journal of Social and Clinical Psychology* 9.

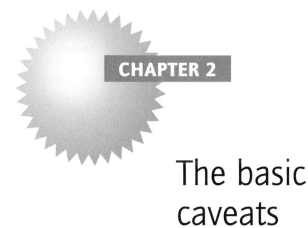

CHAPTER 2

The basic caveats

Some very important basics

As we shall see, body language is not necessarily causal. In a causal relationship 'if A then B' is the result. Hit a golf ball and it will travel in a set direction, reflecting the angle at which the ball was struck, with the distance covered depending on how hard the ball was hit. Causal relation only operates with inanimate objects; in contrast, in body language, just because someone does 'A' it cannot always be interpreted that 'B' will automatically follow; there are many variables and contexts that make up the 'A' in the equation, including the way you react to 'A'.

In fact, body language has no caveats in the formal sense but is rather like a flexible code of practice with lots of exceptions because every human is unique – including yourself and the actual situation. We have deliberately used the word caveat (in Latin, from the present subjunctive 'let him beware') rather than rule or law here.

Before we enter this colourful world of body language, which has a montage of meanings, be aware there are real dangers of misinterpretation. Just like any human activity, there are some aspects which we ignore at our peril.

Caveat 1: Go for clusters

Just as one swallow does not make a summer, so one movement of the body or face in isolation should not be interpreted as having a specific meaning.

If a person touches their nose it can mean, among other things:

- They have an itch.
- They have a pimple.
- They want to breathe through a particular nostril.
- They want to clear one nostril.
- They are nervous.
- They do this all the time when they are happy/nervous/angry (this is known as a 'tic', which we will cover later).

So they are not necessarily telling a lie.

Similarly, a friend might not look you in the eye when they are talking to you because they have found something more interesting to look at; it would be wrong to jump to the conclusion that they are not telling the truth. But, if in addition their behaviour changes and includes a cluster of three or four of the following, then it is almost certain that the friend is just about to deliver what politicians call a 'terminological inexactitude'.

- Body moves suddenly.
- Adam's apple bobs up and down.
- Voice changes in volume and pitch.
- Cough is dry.
- Smile rate increases.
- Blink rate increases.
- Eyebrows clinch.
- Hands move to their mouth.

This is an example of a failed cluster; whilst the man is clapping – a sign of appreciation or recognition – his face is telling another story.

Being able to recognise a cluster of signs will help you understand what is really meant. It is inordinately useful to have a better-than-average chance of knowing when someone is trying influence you in an inappropriate way. It is even more useful to know how to present yourself so that you establish your credibility in what you say.

Most people think that folding arms is a sign of defensiveness. This may be so, but as an activity for yourself, see if you can come up with at least five reasons why someone would want to fold their arms. (Possible reasons are given in Appendix 1 on page 222 at the back of the book.)

However, if the folded arms were accompanied by leaning back in the chair, looking down, tapping their foot and breathing out slowly it would be a safe bet that you were not getting your point across with that individual. Even so, they might just be thinking about the argument they had that morning with their partner!

If you wish to use and comprehend body language, remember
Caveat 1:

Always go for clusters.

Caveat 2: People cannot not communicate

Isn't it interesting that long before you could utter a word you
were able to communicate with and sometimes even control
adults? As has been suggested, communication through formal
language is a very recent phenomena along the long road we
have taken in our evolution. In nature there are complex societies of thousands – ants, bees and even fish – who need no
language to organise their societal way of life. Mammals also
communicate with posture, facial expressions and gaze. So in a
real sense humans are very much communicating animals and
we can choose to use language to express ourselves.

All babies appear gifted to their mothers but all daughters,
whether gifted or not, at about nine months (slightly later
for sons) whilst they might only speak in phonemes or single
syllables still control and communicate with adults! As every
ant, bee and fish knows, you do not have to speak to engineer
a very complex society. Being adults, even if we say nothing,
we can communicate our feelings, desires, dislikes and our
aspirations.

It is an urban legend (because there is no research to support
it) that women usually speak 24,000 words a day; however, from
personal experience my ears tell me it is right. Men speak much
less, around 12,000 words, but these figures are nothing when
compared to the non-verbal word and messages we 'speak' all
the time.

We give and receive tens of thousands of words every day to our partners, friends, work colleagues and strangers without uttering a sound. And this is just with our faces, let alone our bodies and the clothes that adorn them.

Before we think or speak we feel, and when we feel then our bodies move and change to reflect that emotion. We cannot help it and nor can anyone else. As we shall see, if you only listen to the words you might miss 75 per cent of the meaning.

Most of the time our body language is spontaneous, instant, immediate and unconscious, so when you become aware of body language in others you do have a distinct social advantage.

brilliant tip

When you can control as much of your own body language as possible, your advantage is even greater.

Caveat 3: The body finds it difficult to lie

We have already tangentially touched on this in Caveat 1. We can choose our words, we can choose to bluff and be oblique, we can choose to lie, we can even choose not to say anything – a lie of omission – but what is almost impossible for us to do is to hide our true feelings and emotions.

'The eyes of men converse as much as their tongue, with the advantage that the ocular dialect needs no dictionary, but is understood the world over.'

Ralph Waldo Emerson, American philosopher

As adults we know that what people say is not what they mean and sometimes they mean the reverse! How many times have you heard: 'How interesting', 'Fascinating', 'That is so useful, helpful, constructive, lovely...', when you know at best the person is trying to be polite, and at worst drenched in sarcasm that would cut through titanium!

When someone believes in what they are saying and is trying their best to present it well then their body language is likely to be what is called 'congruent' with what they are saying. Should this not be the case then signs will appear in the face, in the body, and in the speed of their voice and thinking time. Always look for congruency. Take a second look at the man on page 5.

It is because of these overt signs that 'we just know' when something is just not right. As one researcher puts it:

'... if the spoken language is stripped away and the only communication left is body language, the truth will find some way of poking through.'[1]

You owe it to yourself not to be taken advantage of or be duped.

Simply put, Caveat 3 means: when someone is speaking or interacting with you, look for congruence between what you hear and what you see. If what you see is different then, if we misquote Mr Speaker, 'the eyes have it'.

Caveat 4: Look for sudden or unexpected changes

Detectives and interrogators are trained to notice sudden changes in a suspect's body movements. Their suspect might be confident and full of bravado one moment then suddenly they might do one or more of the following: tense their body, move back into their chair, shuffle their feet, move their arms across their bodies. The interrogator knows a sensitive issue has been touched on and the suspect requires further questioning.

brilliant example

Also true is the converse situation, in which an innocent suspect being interrogated might show many of the signs of anxiety because they have never been in a police station before as a suspect. Then the detective, knowing that the getaway vehicle was a car, might deliberately lie, saying, 'We have three witnesses that saw you drive off on a motorbike, so it must have been you'. Because the suspect is innocent they are still likely to show all the signs of anxiety. Should they be the actual bank robber there is likely to be a sudden change in their body language. They think to themselves, 'Fantastic! I'm off the hook; the police are obviously misinformed because I drove off in a van'. Immediately they reveal many of the signs of relaxation: their body tenseness vanishes as they stop biting their lip. Possibly a smirk appears on their face and they look at the detective directly in the eyes as if to say, 'Mate, you don't know nothing'. When, in fact, they have just given themselves away.

brilliant tip

Sudden changes in a person's movements nearly always mean something.

Caveat 5: Body language is unique to the individual

Whilst some facial expressions are universal[2] (see page 4), because of our uniqueness and our environments and prevailing culture we develop our own body language style, and in extreme cases these can be what psychologists call 'tics' (see page 181) and poker players call 'tells'. Most husbands will know that unique look their wife makes just before she says something like

'... and another thing', and most wives know when their husbands say their version or variation of 'Yes, dear' that they have not heard a word!

Because of Caveat 3, the more time we spend with someone the better understanding we have of what they really mean when they speak. This is why, even when you reach maturity, you still can't pull the wool over your mother's eyes!

Poker players wear dark glasses so that the dilation of their pupils is concealed to prevent another player being able to gauge the strength or otherwise of the hand they have been dealt. (See page 139.)

brilliant tip

Ask yourself 'What else are they saying besides the words?'

Caveat 6: Context confirms body language

Different social contexts allow for different behaviours. Perhaps like Lawrence of Arabia, a post-meal burp when dining with Bedouins would be appreciated; only an eyebrow might be raised if you did the same while dining at home; but we know that in the Anglo-Saxon company it is a definite no-no if you burp publically.

Placing your first finger and thumb together and making a slight flick of the hand as if you were throwing a dart usually means 'perfect' in the USA and Europe, but in South America it is a very rude sign.

Understanding body language and signs can be likened to mastering a canoe; if you only have the 'sign' paddle on one side you will keep going round in circles. You need the paddle of 'context' on the other side of the canoe and have both pulling together to move forwards towards the pool of comprehension.

Our body language is situational; shaped by our upbringing, our culture, and the demands of whatever is meant by the term 'good manners' and etiquette.

brilliant tip

Ask yourself 'Does the context/culture have a bearing on this?'

brilliant recap

- Always go for body language clusters.
- We cannot help our body language.
- Our body language finds it difficult to lie.
- Sudden body language changes usually mean something.
- Our body language is unique to us.
- Context confirms body language.

So, after this introduction, now we can move on to body language proper, and we start with the distance we like to keep from each other.

References

[1] Fast, J. (1970), *Body Language*.
[2] Ekman, P. (1982), *Emotion in the Human Face*, 2nd edition.

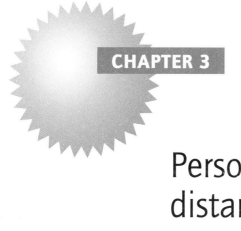

CHAPTER 3

Personal distance or proxemics

Our public, personal and private space

As humans we are very territorial, but we are not usually conscious of this aspect of ourselves until it is invaded or violated. Spatial relationships have an enormous effect on our daily lives.

brilliant definition

Proxemics (noun)

The interrelated observations and theories of man's use of space as a specialised elaboration of culture.

Unwittingly we constantly maintain sovereignty over our space for our own psychological welfare. Just as animals mark out their territory with urine in the hope of achieving privacy, we use furniture, fences and even wedding rings to satisfy the same need. Our need for territorial control and ownership is ubiquitous – we have our favourite chair at home, our table at a restaurant that we frequent, equipment at the gym, and when in church we usually sit in the same pew and show annoyance when someone else dares to sit in 'our' place.

Animals have a fight-flight response; if you encroach on their personal space they will engage in flight, if you cross over into their intimate space they will usually fight.

If a man moves into a woman's personal space, uninvited, she will move away; if he does not take the hint and then moves into her intimate space he can expect a black eye or some significant pain about 45cm lower!

Our personal bubble

It is as if we have an 'ego bubble' that surrounds each one of us and you enter another's bubble at your peril. Powerful people have a larger bubble than the rest of us.

Before we go on to body language proper, it is important to understand that one's personal distance (or proxemics) can have a direct effect on moderating what is not being said non-verbally.

Interpersonal distance communicates acceptance, encouragement or rejection. Put simply – if you like or want to support someone you will move towards them; if you don't, you won't!

brilliant example

We all know the 'laws of lift etiquette', and these five laws have come into existence without any formal legislation or interpersonal training. They are a brilliant example because the limited space in the lift car forces strangers into, for them, an inappropriate social zone:

Law 1

If there are two or more of you then you go straight to your corner and you do not collect £200 but you go to jail and you must stay there until you reach your floor or someone before you reaches theirs.

Law 2

You are forbidden to look another person in the eye or the upper part of their body.

- Males can look where they always look, providing the female is in profile.
- Females can use their superior peripheral vision only to be disappointed that there are no attractive males as fellow travellers. They object to being 'ogled'.

Law 3

If there is a mirror then males can sneak a look at a fellow female traveller by pretending they are adjusting their tie or removing imaginary fluff. If there is no mirror then they have to wait until the female exits the lift.

Law 4

Females travelling more than three floors with another female can, in silence, look at another female's footwear, identify the brand, cost, date they were purchased, whether they are appropriate for the occasion, match the outfit, and finally draw firm conclusions concerning the personality of the wearer before having a serious conversation in their head about whether they approve or not.

Law 5

You can, male or female, concentrate your gaze at the floor and/or the lift indicator light as often as you like.

Where Law 5 may be broken:

- If there is either a baby or a toddler in the lift. This allows positive, polite social comments, smiles and the goo, goo, ga, ga language humans think that babies instinctively comprehend.
- If someone strange – not like the rest of us properly attired people in the lift – joins us we can give knowing looks to each other expressing our superiority over this transient interloper. It is also acceptable to allow a brief smile to someone else should the person in question leave before you do, or to express non-verbal relief.

▶

Social psychologists have a term for this 'distance' behaviour: 'compensatory adjustment'. What is happening here is the fellow lift travellers are creating a comfortable psychological space between themselves.

Should the lift start to make strange mechanical noises and stop halfway between floors the space dynamic would change very quickly because the travellers now all share the same problem and they become an escape team bonded by a common purpose.

The zones of proxemics

Computed by E.T. Hall[1] almost 50 years ago are the four major zones of proximics, as shown in the diagram below:

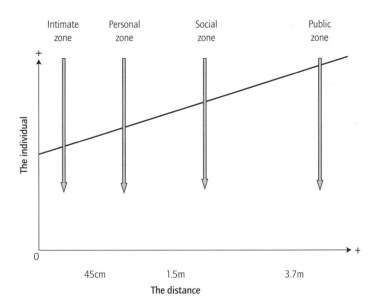

Figure 3.1 The four zones of proxemics.

Intimate zone (15–45cm)

Sometimes called the intimate or the kissing zone, we reserve this for our partners, our children and those to whom we feel very close. In this zone there is bodily contact, appreciation of the other person's personal aroma as well as their body heat. This is the place for cherished sweet whispers and pillow talk.

The intimate zone is beautifully captured in the following:

> 'Only now it had become indispensable to him to have her face pressed close to him; he could never let her go again. He could never let her head go away from the close clutch of his arm. He wanted to remain like that for ever, with his heart hurting him in a pain that was also life to him.'
>
> D.H. Lawrence, *The Horse Dealer's Daughter*

Personal zone (46cm–1.3m)

Here, focused and purposeful eye contact is important. You can also see more of the other person. Touch is possible, but only to those places of the body that are socially acceptable – hands, arms and shoulders – so that touching can be done without entering the intimate zone from a frontal position. When two people stand side by side the personal zone can be reduced.

An example of when the personal zone can become almost intimate because the couple are side on to each other, rather than face to face.

Social zone (1.3–3.5m)

Work and/or work relations are kept in this zone. Again, in this zone visual contact is necessary for interaction and voices are louder. People could easily hear each other in this range with a softer voice but the increase in volume suggests and maintains the formality of the situation. When you pass someone on the pavement you enter the social zone, but you create social distance by looking away.

Public zone (3.6m plus)

Here you can recognise the person and invite them into your social zone with a smile – a smile is easy to recognise from this distance; other nuances of the face are not so easily recognised.

An example of the social zone. What indication is there that the male is not going to be welcome in the female's personal zone? Answer on page 223.

We will see later how one might use these different zones in helping us create rapport, showing that we like or dislike someone, being assertive and influencing others. However, first we need to understand how we see and how we are seen by others.

brilliant recap

- We know instinctively how close we like people to be to us.
- We feel uncomfortable when someone invades our space.
- We show that we like someone by moving closer to them.
- If a smile is reciprocated we have permission to move into the next zone.

Reference

[1] Hall, E. T. (1966), *The Hidden Dimension: Man's Use of Space in Public and Private*.

CHAPTER 4

Perception and first impressions

Beware, what you see is not always what you get!

Our eyes just give us a picture of someone and, as beautiful as they may be, when it comes to what they are really like, our first impression can take us in a wrong direction. In this chapter we examine some of the dangers of first impressions – those we make and those we give.

brilliant definition

Perception (noun)

The recognition and interpretation of sensory input of what you notice in a person when you first see them and then finding meaning by evaluating what you see using your memory of people and what they were like.

(To use the jargon, it is the neurological processes by which such recognition and interpretation are effected. To use ordinary language, from what you see you make 'guestimates' about the person.)

The 7/11 effect

When we meet someone for the first time we want to feel safe and trust that person and we want to do this as quickly as possible. Unfortunately we have little information to go on, so we make judgements on very superficial information – clothing, physical looks, speech, body shape and body language.

Dr Michael Solomon's PhD work at the Graduate School of Business of New York University suggested that when we first meet someone we make 11 – yes, 11 – decisions about a person in the first 7 seconds of contact. The reason for this, I suppose, is that for most of our genetic history as human beings – most of which has been spent swinging around in trees and eating one another – for our own protection we get to sum up strangers very quickly to ensure our survival; are they friend or foe or perhaps lunch or dinner?

Here are the 11 things that we guesstimate about a person:

1 Economic level – where they come in society, how rich or otherwise they are.

2 Educational level – how intelligent they are and what is their probable academic level.

3 How honest and/or credible they are.

4 How much they can be trusted.

5 Their level of sophistication.

6 Gender, their sexual orientation, desirability and availability.

7 Level of success.

8 Political background – how they are likely to vote.

9 Value orientation – whether you share the same values/ principles.

10 Ethnic origin.

11 Social desirability – how much you would like the person as a friend.

If this research is right then just think of the importance of the impression that you will create with an interviewer. How might you wish to strengthen your first impression in line with the position that you are seeking?

Some research suggests that in selection situations interviewers make up their mind about a candidate within the first four minutes.

Later research brings even worse news; now psychologists have better measuring equipment[1] they have determined that it takes not four minutes but just one tenth of a second or 100ms to make a judgement – and that is just by looking at your face!!

Even if this excellent research, which tests credulity, is only partly right then we would do well to reflect and ruminate on the importance of the impression that we create with the people that we meet socially for the first time and, perhaps more importantly, at the job interviews we have as we progress our careers.

If this is not scary enough, these studies then go on to suggest that the remaining time is taken up with trying to discover evidence that will support the original impression! As the old adage goes:

'You don't get a second chance to make a good first impression.'

In most situations, hopefully, as you spend more time with the person you have plenty of opportunity to correct any errors or misunderstandings that may have been formed during those first few seconds of the meeting. In other situations it can be very costly. In an interview situation, where the interviewer has the significant power because they ask the questions, several disadvantages occur if the right impression is not created quickly.

Warning!

When selecting candidates interviewers unwittingly employ what is known as 'selective attention', which includes the following:

- The interviewer has a tendency to ask questions which facilitate answers that only encourage and support their initial impression of you.
- Any information which is contrary to their first impression of you is ignored or discounted.
- Information contrary to the first impression you gave is attributed to the advantages provided by the situation or environment you were in and not to you as an individual.

As soon as we meet another person we judge them and they judge us and most of us have no idea how we come across. This is not because we are ignorant, disinterested or have an ego so large that we do not care, but mostly because after the age of about four years old we are socially trained not to give people feedback – positive or negative.

Sometimes we attempt to project an image which totally fails.

Some people take the position 'what you see is what you get' and I am not going to change, project any other image or make any concession to you, even if it means that you will not want to get into a relationship with me, which will be to my personal detriment because I would like your friendship.

Finally, some people enjoy such a strong ego that they have no comprehension of how egocentric they are and unfortunately display, although unintended, a 'take it or leave it' attitude.

The errors that we can make

Given that we make up our minds very quickly and mainly on the 'physics' of the person, it is little wonder that we are so often wrong. Usually when we are wrong we fall into one of five traps.

We will use the psychological jargon here, for brevity:

Error 1: Temporal extension

The first glance, usually of the face, can be interpreted as an enduring personality trait. If you look stern, happy, anxious or sad then that will be the disposition that you will be given. Remember that assumption about 'Yond Cassius' (see page 48).

If you met this woman for the first time you might think she is a somewhat anxious person because of the way she looks. In fact, the cartoon was based on a very senior politician who is anything but anxious.

Error 2: Parataxis

If you remind the person of someone they know then that person's traits will be transferred to you.

Error 3: Categorisation

You are thought to have the same characteristics as members of a group known to the observer, such as age, ethnicity, gender, etc.

Error 4: Functional quality

Your face, or other parts of it, leads to an interpretation of your personality. Female film starlets have Botox to plump up their lips which is supposed to indicate that they are sexually attractive and active. Young men grow facial hair to make themselves look more mature. Women tie their hair back to look more efficient and they let it down to look more physically appealing.

Error 5: Generalisation

Here your observer will put together several aspects of your appearance and develop a whole theory about you.

Unfortunately for us all we get categorised very quickly, although there is no correlation between that initial impression and our actual personalities. The implications this has when making friends, attending parent teacher nights and even the selection interview are legion. We can't help but generalise when we first meet someone, and that is why so often we realise that our first impressions were so way off base after we get to know the person better.

---

brilliant example

It might be an urban myth, but the actress Maureen Lipman once dressed up as a bag lady and, although she offered the right amount of money at the theatre ticket office, was refused a ticket to her own West End show!

Experiments have shown that members of the public will respond far more positively to a businessman than an itinerant when asked for directions, when in fact it is the same person (an actor) in both situations requesting the same assistance in the same language.

---

brilliant tip

Since we unwittingly also put people into inappropriate boxes, if we are to improve our interpersonal skills the basic rule is:

'Judge people by what they do rather than the way they look.'

brilliant tip

It is vital to start your interview with a very powerful statement about your skills and achievements.

Impression management

If first impressions are this difficult to correct or amend, creating the right impression becomes an essential part of anyone's interpersonal armory.

brilliant definition

Impression management (noun)

The way in which a person, by controlling as many aspects of their behaviour as possible, may wish to be seen by another or others in an attempt to influence them to accept the persona being proffered.

Research suggests that the more attractive you are (see what we say about symmetry on page 131) the more favourably you are judged on a whole host of parameters, but here we cover some tactics that you can employ to manage your first impression.

Obviously, taking Solomon's research seriously (the 7/11 effect – see page 35) there is not much we can do about ethnicity or gender, but we can do much about our social desirability and how honest we appear. So here are the basics, many of which we shall revisit in detail when we come to rapport skills:

- Maintain social eye contact – it shows confidence, credibility and honesty.
- Smile – it shows personal warmth and friendship.
- Initiate the handshake – it shows confidence and warmth.
- Nod slightly on meeting – it shows respect.
- Put your shoulders in parallel – it shows friendship and confidence.
- Point your feet towards the other person – it shows friendship and confidence.
- Lean forward when you speak – it shows friendship and interest.
- Mirror the other person's body language – it will increase trust and rapport.

There are many other things we can do to achieve a favourable impression, and we turn to those now.

Dress appropriately

Animals communicate to each other by making variations in the colour of their fur, while birds adjust their overall colouring. In the same way our dress is not just for comfort and/or protection, and for some it makes a deliberate statement. After the person's face the second thing we notice and interpret is the way they are dressed.

Are we all like birds?

'Birds of a feather flock together', so the saying goes, and this is also true for people. It is a natural response to tend to be suspicious of people who are not like us. It is easier to be accepted as an individual when others are comfortable in your presence. We should note that this is not strictly body language, since the way we adorn our bodies is a conscious decision. However, it is important to do as much as you can to blend into the environment of the other person(s) if that is your wish. Teenagers lead fashion because most up-and-coming generations want to look different to their parents and adults.

We communicate through the way we dress in a whole variety of ways – including gender, with men buttoning their clothes from left to right from the days when we had to draw our swords quickly. Women, it is said, traditionally buttoned from right to left so they could suckle their child and achieve some modicum of modesty.

We can express our financial and political orientation by what we wear. The great political strategist Machiavelli, way back in 1513, urges the Prince always to wear his best if he is to be respected and feared.

Mark Twain rightly suggested in the 1880s:

'Clothes make the man.'

He then went on to suggest, after thinking about it, the more pertinent but not so well-known corollary:

'Naked people have little or no influence on society.'

Dress to impress

So, think about the way you dress. Does what you are wearing support who you are, or want to be, or the impression you like people to have of you?

Every experienced judge is aware that criminal barristers ensure their (male) clients enter the dock clean-shaven, wearing a dark suit, decent white shirt and a sober tie in the hope of a lighter sentence.

Of course, all of us can dress in whatever way we like, but what we wear does have social implications.

So clothes are the big guns of impression management. When we meet someone for the first time, after looking at the face, an extensive clothes' evaluation immediately takes place. Research suggests that men, in rank order, look at a women's clothing third, with the top and second position going to face and figure respectively.[2]

Clothes can also show off one's physique, for men, and figure, for women, as well as suggest, for both sexes, sexual availability, in addition to covering up narrow shoulders in a man or uplifting a small bust for a female.

Perhaps the strictest dress codes are in the armed services, where all personnel wear the same colour but their individual status is reflected on their cap, lapel, shoulder and cuff.

Dress reflects the cloning mechanism in us all. The higher you go in management in a particular organisation, the stronger the cloning with regard to dress. Look at almost any annual report where there is the mandatory photograph of the smiling board members. Usually they are all wearing the same type of clothes in the same colours. Hair styles, too, tend to be the same. One tip here might be that to dress for success, dress like your boss's boss.

So little of us is displayed

One of the more important questions that selectors ask of themselves, once you have proved your competence for the position and how motivated you are, is: 'Will this person fit in?' The decision is highly influenced by the way that you are dressed. This is not unreasonable, given that men only reveal 12 per cent of their bodies and a woman wearing a skirt rather than trousers displays 17.5 per cent. With the remaining percentage we make a statement.

For females this is particularly apposite when being considered for executive positions. However, for low-status positions how you dress has no marked influence on how you are viewed.[3]

brilliant tip

Where you need to be socially accepted, including at work, create the right impression by dressing one level up – two levels if you can afford it and carry it off. On the other side of the coin, if you dress differently to your adopted clan or the one to which you aspire, then there are immediate acceptance, and at work, possible promotion difficulties.

But I am an individual!

You may think that individuality is important but it can be interpreted as 'I don't care' or, worse, 'I am ignorant of the fact that dress is important'. Both in social and work situations this is definitely an important decision one should think carefully about before making a grand individual sartorial statement.

brilliant example

Chairpersons and presidents of not-for-profit organisations are the exception here. They do not have to impress anybody in the organisation so they can wear the colourful tie or a scarf French-style to express their individuality. Americans call this 'fluffing out'. Notice, though, that when the chairperson addresses the shareholder meeting they may revert to the standard executive uniform and this applies too for the president at the society's AGM.

brilliant tips

Remember what was said about birds of a feather (see page 42)? The overriding rule here for success is to dress in the style of your boss's boss (even if your boss is a different gender to yourself they will have a certain style) so that you look like one of the top flock. Here are 14 tips for work that might also help, depending on your situation:[4]

1   No more than two colours or two patterns for your outfit is almost mandatory.

2   Be fashionable but conservative in clothes, shoes and hairstyle – unless you are in the creative business.

3   No jewellery for men, apart from a wedding ring and/or a signet ring.

4   Dress as expensively as you can afford – but do not flash expensive brands.

5   Darker and solid colours make you look more powerful than lighter colours and patterns.

6   Co-ordinate your colours.

7   Do some research and see what other successful people are wearing in your profession or function – professional magazines are good for this.

8   Do not stint on accessories – remember that a cheap watch, ballpoint pen or handbag will ruin the image of even the most expensive outfit.

9   Invest in a decent pen and do not use those cheap instruments that you have 'stolen' from your current employer.

10 Men – especially engineers and research boffins: for the interview you only need one pen, kept on the inside of your jacket, not ten pens standing like soldiers in your shirt pocket.

11 Men over 50: get a good haircut and trim facial hair – and I am not talking about your chin!

12 If you don't have a decent watch then leave that at home too; at the other end of the scale, if the watch is a gold Rolex or an Omega, leave that in the safe at home because they will think that they will not be able to afford you – unless you are at the kind of level where such an item is almost a mandatory part of the executive 'uniform'.

13 If you must carry an attaché case to work, make sure that it is thin, in good condition and contains nothing except the essentials for your work. (The basic rule is the thicker your case the lower you are in the organisation – CEOs are able to carry nothing because others do it for them.)

14 Women: your call, but over-femininity may prevent you breaking the glass ceiling and you are likely to remain on the female stick floor of your organisation.

'Clothes don't make the man, but clothes have got many a man a good job.'

Herbert Vreeland

For political aspirants – could it help you if you adopted a distinguishable outfit and/or accessories? If appropriate, and if you need to stand out from your ambitious rivals, you could always wear the same outfit or accessory (actually, buy several of the same outfit, for reasons of hygiene, but they must be identical). Examples would include: Stalin (workers' overalls), Mao Zedong (Red Star cap), Churchill (pinstripes and that cigar), Wilson (pipe), Thatcher (wearing blue), Hussein (pistol), Castro (beard and cap) and Gaddafi and Arafat (traditional dress). Finally, Boris – who could forget that hairstyle or that bike?

This also works for pop stars and soccer heroes.

The face

When we get close to someone for the first time we look to the face because it is the largest data bank of non-verbal communication. Our faces 'speak' by what they are doing – even babies can say 'No' by shaking their heads – and, because of stereotyping, might on occasion communicate personality.

'Yond Cassius has a mean and hungry look,
He thinks too much. Such men are dangerous.'

Julius Caesar, Act I, Scene II.

Genetically we are programmed to like and find attractive those people who are fit. Unfortunately for those whose body shape is endomorph (plump, cuddly, full, generous, etc.), life is not fair yet again. The world is prejudiced against those who are seen to be fat; most large people already know this through comments made about them at school and the interview opportunities lost. All this discrimination and unfairness is supported by researchers such as Linda Lin, a psychologist professor of Emmanuel College in the USA, whose research focuses on obesity and prejudice against the obese.

Maybe people are hard-wired to know intuitively that excess fat in the abdominal region poses a greater health risk than excess fat in the hips and thighs, but the facts are that such a body shape invites a higher risk of high blood pressure, diabetes, early onset of heart disease, and certain types of cancers. This might be statistically true, but remember what Disraeli said about statistics: 'There are lies, damned lies, and statistics.' Ultimately, the best tip here is that you should aim to achieve your ideal body weight.

Hair

T. S. Eliot's J. Alfred Prufrock was absolutely right to be concerned about being progressively follicly challenged, as hair gives a clear indication of age. As we grow older our hair loses both its thickness and its strength. Androgenic alopecia is the fancy name for this and consequently it is difficult for older men (and some women) to have long hair. In the USA 25 per cent of men begin to go bald by the age of 30 and 66 per cent by the time they are 60.

It is common knowledge that the propensity to go bald is directly related to age, but it is interesting to note that both males and females associate baldness with social maturity and being less aggressive.[5] If you have a beard, which is a secondary sexual signal, then depending on the culture this can be associated with virility and wisdom.

Although hair length is determined and greatly influenced by fashion, it has been suggested that men with short hair are rated as more masculine (of course, because traditionally women have long hair) and competent (which is not obvious!). So, if you're a man – short hair wins!

It is more difficult to work either at a desk, in a court room or at a machine with your masculine locks flowing down – and less hygienic, of course, because long hair demands far more attention to maintain and keep clean.

Research shows that American attorneys with short hair win more cases, and this is attributed to looking more competent with less locks. So it is useful for British barristers to maintain that eighteenth-century wig after all![6]

brilliant example

For females the message is the same. Women with shorter hair are thought to be more professional – think Superwoman before she lets her hair down with an exaggerated swing and flick of her head. Even Virgin Air, which prides itself on not being stuffy but trendy and friendly, encourages their female flight attendants to have their hair 'off their collars'.

As we all know, as a secondary sex indicator men have more body and facial hair and sometimes this breaks into fashion. It has become rare now to see an advert showing a man who is clean shaven in a young man's fashion magazine – and much female private time and money is taken up with removing their bodily hair for the same reasons.

There is some research that suggests that a major change in hairstyle can be made after a significant and stressful emotional event. Men grow or take off beards; women change their hair style or colour. Again, we all know of exceptions to this, but it is surprising how often this happens.

Personal hygiene

This is so obvious but it does need a brief mention. Clean hands, nails, hair and face are critical to health, so any aberration here will mark you down immediately. This is an area where women fare much better than men, who often slip up in this vital part of making an appropriate first impression.

However, there is one area where women rather than men might make a mistake and that is in using an inappropriate perfume that does not complement their natural aroma. Because the individual aroma of another is picked up subconsciously, the perfume might dominate rather than complement. In other words, they will smell just like the perfume and not like themselves with perfume.

'Less is more' would appear to be the rule here; musky and sweet perfumes are heavy scents and thus can be interpreted as aggressive. By the same token, floral perfumes are more appropriate for a date than for everyday use. Apparently lavender and other aromatics give the impression of restfulness and taking things easy. People who are expert in these areas suggest citrus or fruity perfumes give the impression of energy and action.

brilliant recap

- Always check your first impressions – look for hard evidence.
- Dress to impress and wear clothes that will match the image you wish to present.
- Get to your ideal weight – looking fit is always attractive.
- Go easy on the perfume/aftershave.
- Hair at work – men, keep it short; women, keep it off the collar.

Now we have jumped the first hurdle in forming relationships we must turn to the second: how to control our natural anxiety.

References

[1] Willis, J. and Todorov, A. (2006), 'First impressions: Making up your mind after 100ms exposure to a face', *Psychological Science* 17.

[2] Knapp, M. L. and Hall, J. A. (2006), *Nonverbal Communication in Human Interaction*.

[3] Glick, P. et al. (2005), *Psychology of Women Quarterly* 29 (4).

[4] Eggert, M. (1992), *The Perfect Interview: All you need to get it right first time*.

[5] Muscarella, F. and Cunningham, M. R. (2001), 'The evolutionary significance and social perception of male pattern baldness and facial hair', *Ethology and Sociobiology* 17.

[6] Edward, D. and Joseph, R. (1999), *Brief Writing and Oral Argument*.

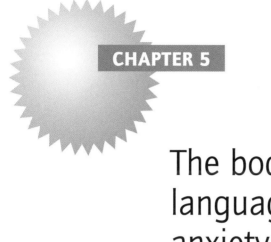

CHAPTER 5

The body language of anxiety

We all have it

Everyone at some time in their life experiences anxiety, and it has many behavioural, cognitive and emotional components. In this chapter we shall concentrate on the somatic elements or the way in which our bodies manifest stress. Anxiety, unless it is a clinical condition, is usually brought on by something specific, which is most often one of four reasons:

1   A current event for which your resources are inadequate.

2   A significant future event not experienced before.

3   A previous experience which was painful and closure has not occurred.

4   A future event which was painful the last time it was experienced.

---

brilliant example

How would you feel if you went to the dentist and as you opened your mouth they said: 'Oh dear, I have not seen one of these before. Goodness, it does look nasty'? The dentist takes a deep breath and says: 'Oh well, I suppose I just have to get on with it; now just relax, I don't think this is going to hurt you too much!'

This hits all 1–4 of the reasons for anxiety (see previous page).

We tend to stress not about the things in the past which we have overcome, but those yet to happen in the future, even if the likelihood of the event occurring is low.

brilliant definition

Anxiety (noun)

A psychological and physical state which has behavioural, emotional, cognitive (thinking) and somatic (bodily) aspects. These components unite to create feelings such as deep concern, fear, negative apprehension and / or uneasiness. It is usually brought about by negative thinking about future events, sometimes based on previously painful events personally experienced or observed.

However, anxiety is not always a bad thing. Anxiety, like arousal, can sometimes drive us into successful action to ensure that what we think might happen is postponed or terminated by pre-emptive behaviour.

Now we are going to cover some more specific indicators of anxiety, but first it is helpful if we dip into some of our evolutionary history.

Lessons from the cave

When we were swinging around in trees and living in caves it was quite an idyllic life, working just 14 hours a week to feed ourselves and our family. Then we became aware of the sabre-toothed tiger stalking us. Suddenly, without you even having to think about it, the hypothalamus in your brain shouts down to the adrenal glands and almost immediately you become Superman, in that you can bite, jump, hit, run, and even think quicker than you could five minutes before. The blood vessels near your skin drain, ensuring minimum blood loss if bitten, while your heart rate doubles, sending extra blood to your muscles so you can fight or flee. Your vision is also improved by the increased dilation of your pupils. At the same time, almost every function of your body that is not required to help you escape or fight is reduced significantly or dispensed.

In evolution our bodies adapt very slowly, and although fortunately today there are no sabre-toothed tigers to treat us like a hamburger on legs, we still get just as anxious and our bodies still respond in much the same way as those of our early humanoid ancestors. Physical signs of stress appear very quickly – most of them without you knowing and most you cannot control, particularly your heart rate and sweating. Now comes the vicious circle: you do not wish to appear nervous so you do your very best to control your nerves, which increases your stress, and the harder you try, the more you sweat, the more you breathe. Then you begin to shake, and as you try to control the shakes the more you … All the very opposite of what you wish to do and how you would like to appear to others.

Here, then, are some of the major body language hints that someone is anxious.

Self-touching

When we were small children and we were upset, in pain or frightened, our parents, usually our mothers, would hold, pat and stroke us to comfort and protect us. Guess what? Without our mothers being present we do it to ourselves, and especially to our faces. In extremes we might cover our eyes or our mouths – signs of attempting to protect ourselves – but in normal work circumstances we would touch our chins, our ears, and the sides of our faces in an attempt to comfort ourselves. This is one of the most unconscious movements that we make. We realise or can remember that we smiled or nodded or gestured but not that we self-touched.[1] When considering self-touching[2] it is important to note that these non-verbal communications can also suggest other emotions, so one has to remember Caveat 1 of the basic body language caveats ('Go for clusters': see page 14).

Not too dissimilar to this, when under pressure, is lip biting, which is in effect an attempt to hold on to your mouth with your upper teeth. It is a phenomenon particularly evident in inexperienced presenters and public speakers.

The grooming exception

However, there is a very important exception to self-touching which, in social situations, you might miss to your cost. This is when we find someone else attractive; it is here that we begin to groom ourselves, usually beginning with touching our hair. Subconsciously we are attempting to make ourselves more attractive so that we are looking our best to the other person. It is a way of saying 'I find you attractive and I hope you find me just as attractive too'. The good news here is if they mirror you (see page 88) by then grooming themselves they hope that you find them attractive too, and thus begins the relationship dance.

Facial giveaways

Anxiety or fear visible in the face is one of the six facial expressions universally recognised among all cultures.[3] In work situations we more than likely want to hide this face and the most common strategy is to smile, but unfortunately in such situations it is difficult to conjure up a natural smile. Remember what we said about body language 'leaking' out.

Blinking

A new branch of psychology called psychophysiology[4] looks at the relationship between mood and physical state and the signs

No prizes for who is disapproving of what he is hearing and who wants to say something. The man on the right is holding himself back and more than likely he is not conscious of what his body language is saying.

that the body gives out. We normally blink at a rate of between 14 and 16 blinks per minute, depending on lighting, the dryness of the air, temperature levels, other environmental factors and what we are doing at the time. What is interesting here is that when under pressure our blink rate changes significantly.

brilliant example

President Clinton has many clips on YouTube; watch any one and then watch the clip where he is denying his relationship with Monica Lewinski. Pay attention to the significant change and increase in his blink rate, showing that even US Presidents, who should be well practised in controlling their body language when delivering 'terminological inexactitudes', still cannot control leakage in their non-verbal behaviour.

Note: *There is a condition called blepharospasm where some unfortunate people – twice as many women as men – have blink spasms due to an involuntary muscle contraction. Unlike some forms of stuttering, a spasm can occur at any time and thus is no indication of anxiety or stress.*

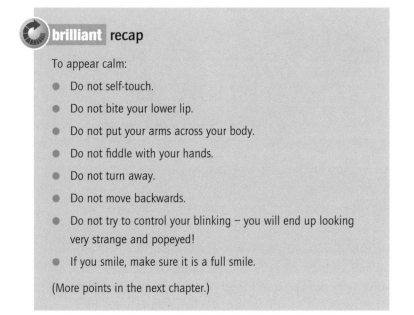

brilliant recap

To appear calm:

● Do not self-touch.

● Do not bite your lower lip.

● Do not put your arms across your body.

● Do not fiddle with your hands.

● Do not turn away.

● Do not move backwards.

● Do not try to control your blinking – you will end up looking very strange and popeyed!

● If you smile, make sure it is a full smile.

(More points in the next chapter.)

References

[1] Murphy, J. A. and Schmid, N. A. (2007), 'Non-verbal self-accuracy in interpersonal interaction', *Personality and Social Psychology Bulletin* 33.

[2] Goldberg, S. and Rosenthal, R. (1986), 'Self-touching behavior in the job interview: Antecedents and consequences', *Journal of Nonverbal Behavior* 10 (1).

[3] Ekman, P. (1982), *Emotion in the Human Face*, 2nd edition.

[4] Stern, J. (1988), 'What's behind blinking? The mind's way of punctuating thought', *The Sciences* 28 (6).

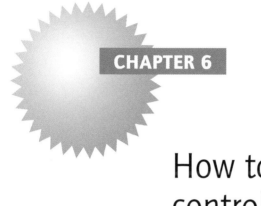

CHAPTER 6

How to
control anxiety

Making our butterflies fly in formation

Because our true feelings leak out so quickly and our anxiety is genuine, control here is difficult, but there are some strategies that we can employ – more like camouflage rather than eradication.

Here I quote extensively from a graduation speech given at Sydney University.[1]

---

brilliant example

I once heard about a study of anxiety levels in paratroopers. What the researcher did was to attach an instrument to people parachuting out of planes. This instrument measured anxiety levels, heart rate, breathing rate and so on. There was a little clock in this mechanism in order to get correlations between changes in anxiety and what was happening at that moment.

What the researcher discovered in this study was that, for the first-time jumpers, when the instruction was given to get into the plane the anxiety went up; when the plane took off the anxiety got higher; when the announcement was made as they were approaching the jump sight the anxiety got higher still; when the door was opened on the plane the anxiety got higher; and finally when the person actually jumped – acute anxiety.

For the veteran jumpers – that is, those who had jumped many many times – when they got into the plane, no anxiety; plane takes off, no anxiety;

approaching the jump sight, no anxiety; open the door of the plane, no anxiety; the jump, no anxiety; but just before they hit the ground, anxiety would go up.

And the researcher interpreted the data this way: the veteran jumpers knew, by experience, that you never get hurt jumping out of the plane – it is the 'damn ground you've got to watch out for'!

---

brilliant tip

Only be anxious about the thing than can really harm you, physically or emotionally.

Now let's cover the body language examples.

Coughing and lip licking

More people – about three out of every four – have a fear of speaking in public which is far greater than necrophobia, arachnophobia, achluophobia and acrophobia (fear of death, spiders, darkness and heights respectively, which are the others in the top five of fears). Interestingly, maybe because traditionally men make more presentations in public than women, it is the men who more frequently seek treatment to overcome fear of public speaking, or perhaps it is because women are just naturally far more fluent.[2]

Have you experienced or seen someone make a presentation during which the points they make are interspersed with hollow coughs? Anxiety tightens the throat muscles and breathing is quickened, both having the effect of drying the throat and our speech equipment. In particular the working of the saliva glands change, making you want to cough. The process also makes us want to lick our lips.

One can also notice a man's body language cluster: his Adam's apple bounces up and down and with two fingers he covers his mouth, almost touching the base of his nose with them.

Experienced public speakers, such as politicians and clergymen, hardly ever cough when speaking or preaching – if they do it could be a sure sign that they are on shaky ground, which is making them anxious.

Note: Just as some childhood behaviours persist into adulthood, lip biting can become an entrenched habit and may not be an unconscious sign of body language communication but what we would call a 'tic'. (See more on vocal and other tics on page 180.)

brilliant tips

1   Practise, practise what you are going to say until you know it so well you do not have to think 'What am I going to say next?'

2   When questioned or challenged, use 'the politician's padding'. Because the brain can work much faster than the way you speak, you only need a little time, i.e. a little padding, so that you can get your brain into gear. For example:

Question:

'Why do you say that?'

Your answer:

'Thank you so much for your question because it is a very important part of what I want to say, and no doubt there are others in the room who are thinking along similar lines as your good self. I deliberately mentioned and emphasised that particular interesting point because ...'

All the above is padding and it takes about 15 seconds to deliver this introduction to your response – more than enough time for your brain to find a suitable answer.

Laughter and the half smile

Some laughter provides a distinct relief for the individual. We laugh when we see clowns engaging in slapstick routines at which, if they were part of real life, we would be horrified. In a way we are laughing as a relief that what we are seeing is fortunately not actually happening to ourselves.

Similarly, giving only half a smile (the mouth moves but nothing happens above the nose) usually indicates nervousness. We are trying to placate our antagonist by saying, in 'body speak', 'I recognise that you are more powerful than me so please do not hurt me'. In just the same way, a dog will go over on to its back and reveal its tummy.

A half smile can be interpreted as anxiety. Our faces are trying to be nice to the perceived aggressor, saying, 'Let's be friends, please do not hurt me'. (Leonardo da Vinci's Mona Lisa is, of course, a famous exception to this rule.)

A half smile can also be a 'micro expression' which appears on our faces for less than one-fiftieth of a second and can be a sign of nervousness. Our only advantage here is that these micro expressions, unless you have had training, are only recognised by 10 per cent of the population.[3]

brilliant tips

1 If you begin to feel anxious, keep a straight face and do not be tempted to smile or, worse, giggle.
2 Do not touch your face.

Perspiration

Perspiration in a social setting is usually not acceptable unless you are an athlete in training or a singer under all those stage lights. But we cannot stop ourselves perspiring and glowing, especially when we are anxious.

We have most sweat glands on our faces and palms; although interestingly our palms do not sweat when we are hot – palm sweat glands only react when we are emotionally stressed and these will work overtime when we feel threatened or emotionally challenged. How many of us have begun to perspire in a wonderfully air-conditioned office when we begin to make a presentation to our peers or superiors?

brilliant tip

Let the handkerchief in your pocket be your best friend. When you use it, leave your hand in your pocket for a while as it will present a more casual (confident) look.

Blading and body movement

Depending on whether we wish to be aggressive (fight) or submissive (flight) our bodies respond differently. When being submissive we turn to the side, which in self-defence jargon is called 'blading', thereby exposing as little of our bodies as possible. In most situations in life we are not likely to be physically hit, but this caveman response, though somewhat less pronounced, still occurs even if it is just our feet pointing at the door or towards a possible escape route. We also move backwards, increasing our distance from the other person. Even when sitting, as we would during an interview, candidates physically move backwards in their chairs when challenged with a question such as 'I see that you do not have an MBA'. Not that the challenge matters anyway, otherwise why would the interviewer be seeing you if not having an MBA was a deal breaker? Probably the challenge is just to see how you will respond to the question, since being challenged and responding well is an essential competency required in the position.

Here the male has moved almost into the intimate zone. In response, the woman, whilst perhaps not being able to give 'the cold shoulder', is showing her true feelings with the direction of her feet.

When we are anxious and trying to get away our bodies provide us with extra energy to do so. However, if we cannot remove ourselves from the situation, that energy, because it is difficult to contain, seeps out and we tap our feet, move our bodies and our arms and rub our fingers together, but not in a natural way.

Looking confident

In this section we will start with the body, then the face, then move on to 'exuding confidence'. As we will see again and again, much of our body language is instinctive and it occurs without us even knowing.

Body

If you are under threat physically it is silly to keep your body square on to your opponent because you make yourself more vulnerable. In martial arts participants are taught to 'blade' their bodies (see page 67) so that they are side on to the opponent, almost looking over their shoulder. Boxers do the same. In this way you are protecting yourself by providing less of a target for your opponent.

What is interesting is that if you are attacked psychologically or find yourself in a fearful situation the body naturally 'blades' itself. Many a presentation has been given with the feet placed in a 'ten-to-four' stance rather than 'ten-to-two'. Irrespective of what the individual is saying, even if it is delivered with conviction and enthusiasm, his or her body is saying: 'I feel so nervous I would rather not be here'.

brilliant tip

Do not concede your space or ground: keep your feet pointed towards the person and make sure your shoulders are parallel with theirs.

The eyes have it

As anxiety increases so the eyes spend less time in eye contact and more time taking in the surrounding area, presumably to note opportunities to flee or to escape.

We can take a second chance at looking at someone by looking askance. This also requires the shoulders to move in the same direction as the eyes. We also look askance when we perceive that the person may be a threat to us, either physically or verbally.

In conflict situations eye contact can be taken as aggressive behaviour, and so eyes are averted. Eyes are also averted or cast down in the presence of perceived individuals of power or rank; in China, for example, it was traditionally an offence to look upon the countenance of the Emperor.

As already mentioned, we need clear eyes to see the way out of trouble so our blink rate also increases with stress and anxiety. Not that we count each other's blink rates but we just 'know' when there is something out of the ordinary happening.

brilliant tips

1   If you are anxious about looking someone in the eye, just look between their eyebrows and they will not know the difference.

2   In large presentations identify four attendees, one in each quadrant of the room, and deliver your presentation just to them, looking at each one in a random order. Presenting to four people is far less anxious-making than looking at 400!

The mouth

Have you ever noticed the interesting phenomenon that when under pressure people can tend to giggle and laugh? In these situations it is a half laugh because it only involves the mouth and not the eyes.

You can tell when someone is not used to or does not like giving a speech or presentation; their throat closes up, their mouth becomes dry and as an attempt to improve things they either swallow (men have a bigger Adam's apple so it is more difficult for them to hide this) or cough. Sometimes people will bite their lips as if they are attempting to prevent themselves speaking, which is the very opposite of what they are supposed to be doing.

When anxious, our mouths do strange things like dry up very quickly, which causes changes in our voice and also causes us to lick our lips – a sure sign of nervous anxiety.

How were we comforted when we were under the age of six months? We were given the breast, bottle or dummy. How do some of us comfort ourselves in stressful situations? We put things in our mouths – cigarettes, chewing gum, ends of pens, the ear piece from our glasses and, of course, our fingernails. This might be a habit which we indulge in on a daily basis, but the rate at which we put things in our mouth increases in line with the level of experienced anxiety. It is as if keeping the mouth busy somehow reduces the stress level – perhaps it is an alternative to 'comfort food'.

brilliant tips

1 Have a glass of water handy and sip it as soon as you feel nervous.

2 If you normally wear glasses you can look very professorial by sucking the end of them, giving the impression that you are thinking rather than trying to get some saliva into your mouth!

Just keep breathing

Yes, we all do it, but how we do it and how often is an indication of our confidence level. Breathing is something we do not usually think about – it just happens because we do not need to think to make it happen. When confident breathing takes place at an unconscious level it is slow and regular. When we are anxious our air intake speeds up considerably as we take quick shallow breaths. In fact, we can increase our rate of breathing by about 40 per cent, getting lots of oxygen into our muscles and preparing ourselves for fight or flight.

Combined with breathing, the nose can also flare to maximize air intake, but more commonly a flared nose is a sign of anger, when we need more air to be able to fight.

Psychologists use a technique called 'breathing in threes' in therapy to teach their clients to overcome stress.

brilliant activity

Try breathing in threes. Breathe and hold your breath whilst counting to three, then breathe out, again slowly counting to three.

Do this breathing activity five times and then become aware of your bodily reaction. Instruct a friend to do this, without telling them why, and ask them how it makes them feel. This is particularly useful if you wish to appear confident, if you are under stress, or you just wish to appear confident before an activity.

Keep your hands still

When our confidence fails our hands go into action. They provide comfort, touching those places where perhaps our mothers touched us in order to provide comfort – we will touch or stroke our cheeks or our hair (see page 57). It is not because we itch or need to groom, but rather to comfort ourselves when we feel under pressure.

When sitting down we might cross our legs and fold our arms. The latter, of course, can be not only a sign of defensiveness but also opposition, as if you are saying, 'Go on, impress me if you can'.

On hearing bad news or seeing something which is painful to us we will instinctively protect ourselves by using our hands to cover our ears, or sometimes our mouth or forehead, as we say 'Oh, no!' In fact, through our body language we are trying to block the unwanted information.

Young babies automatically grip when frightened and as adults this tendency is still with us – we talk about 'white-knuckle rides' at the fairground where we are frightened so much by the adventure ride that we hold on tightly so that our knuckles literally go white. As previously revealed, a significant fear for most adults is speaking in public, so when we have to speak we display our white knuckles as we grip the lectern or the table from which we are delivering our speech.

brilliant tips

How to exude confidence whilst sitting

1 Sitting on the edge of your chair shouts 'I'm anxious' and forces you at first to sit upright, and then as time elapses slowly you begin to slouch as your spine collapses. Neither pose exudes confidence. If you sit on the edge of the chair and you begin to relax it not only makes you look a physical wreck but also gives the impression of total boredom and disinterest. Place your bottom in the back of the chair and just relax; let the back of the chair support you as you maintain a good posture and place your hands on your lap. Under no circumstances touch your face, and try to ignore any itch that you may have if you can.

This last position also has the advantage of allowing you to add emphasis when you want to make a point or say something to the group. This is the strategy: straighten your back slightly and lean forward, place the inside of your wrists on the table and steeple (see page 168) but move your hands in a natural way when you want to illustrate or emphasise a point. Moving into the space of the discussion shows both confidence and friendliness. (Moving from one zone to another – see page 28 – was one of the earliest body language signs noted by psychologists.[4]) Begin speaking as you move forward and if there is a debate about what you are saying then stay in that position. Once you have made your point, finished your answer or the discussion has moved on, that is the time to move back to your original sitting position. More on this later – see page 165.

▶

2   Interlock your fingers so that it looks like steepling and so that you appear relaxed, or just sit on your hands. This might sound silly, but one usually sits at a table and so what you do with your hands cannot be seen.

brilliant recap

- Breathe slowly.
- Stand tall and square up to the individual or your audience.
- Look at the person(s) with whom you are in conversation, or if you are giving a presentation then scan your audience.
- Steeple your hands – i.e. interlock your fingers.
- If you really need to hold on to something, lock your wrists behind your back from time to time. The fact that you are confident enough to display your body might just do the trick.
- If your throat dries, have a glass of water handy.
- Before you begin, take some large breaths and then breathe slowly throughout your presentation.

References

[1] Corlett, A. (2009), lecture given at Sydney University by a member of the External Advisory Committee, Department of Government and International Relations, Faculty of Arts, 9 October 2009.

[2] Keyes, S. (1983), 'Sex differences in cognitive abilities', *Journal of Sex Roles* 9 (8).

[3] Ekman, P. (2003), *Emotions Revealed*.

[4] James, W. T. (1932), 'A study of the expression of bodily posture', *Journal of General Psychology* 7.

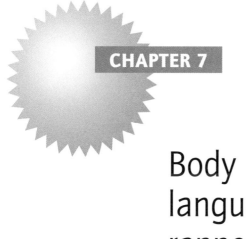

CHAPTER 7

Body language for rapport skills

Becoming bodylingual

Rapport is the door to any relationship – if it cannot be opened and kept open then the relationship just fails to flourish. It also has a role to play in adversarial situations such as a negotiation and is certainly essential if you wish to persuade someone to your point of view.

In everyday language rapport is about getting 'in sync' with another person; it is ensuring that the other person feels comfortable in your presence and not in any way threatened. Rapport is the beginning of trust between two people and needs to be maintained for the duration of the relationship – this is sometimes known as 'personal unfolding'.[1]

This is where Mehrabian's 55 per cent becomes so important (see page 7). Spend some time where people meet and chat to each other and immediately you will notice who is in rapport and who is not – the difference is in their body language. Those in rapport are matching each other in the way in which they move their bodies; 'It is a dance of mutual response.'[2] The deeper the rapport, the stronger the matching of the body language of both people.

We will deal with this aspect in some detail towards the end of the chapter, but first let us examine those aspects that we can control directly in our 'new' relationships when we first meet someone.

Much of the body language associated with rapport is covered elsewhere. As it is such a vital aspect it is worth indulging in some of what we have covered before here, but I have also given it an additional slant.

So, to repeat the basics: relax as much as you can, establish social eye contact and create symmetry in your body, which also shows that you are confident and relaxed in a person's presence, and, finally, smile. We smile at people we like – and if you really want to go overboard you can raise your eyebrows as you do so. (See page 82 for the components of a real smile.)

In addition to these basics, nod your head whenever you can agree with the speaker.[3] It is very easy to do and conveys warmth, agreement and pleasantness to the other person, and who does not want to get into rapport with someone who exudes these friendly characteristics?

Whilst talking of head nods it has also been found that if you tip your head to one side you can change someone's impression of you from arrogant and unsociable to kind and thoughtful – it even makes you look more trustworthy[4] – but note, for best results, tilt to the right.

The origins of rapport

The origins of rapport skills go way back into our prehistory as humans to when it was a very important survival skill to show that you were not a threat. It is also important for us to know if we are under threat, so the ability to scan the body language of another in days of old was, and still is, a very useful skill. As a consequence of our tens of thousands of years of social heritage, much of our rapport body language is not part of our conscious awareness and has moved from being a survival technique to being a social function. Yes, we live in the twenty-first century, but scrape the surface and we are still in our close-knit tribes. Today the 'Old Boy' network is alive and well in a whole host of disguises, demonstrating the same values, speech patterns, personal preferences and clothes!

Skills of rapport can almost be summed up in one word: mimicry. Not only do birds of a feather flock together, but so too do humans, casting doubt on the adage that opposites attract. The more you can be like the other person, the greater will be the possibility of creating rapport. This works in all sorts of ways, many of them pioneered in the area of body language by Richard Bandler and John Grinder of NLP fame.[5]

People who are in rapport mirror their body positions (see page 88); they use the same type of gestures and facial expressions. In a real sense they are conversing in the same body language. Go anywhere where people meet one another and spend some time observing them: it becomes immediately apparent that people have their shoulders in parallel, their bodies move almost together, and they look at each other at the same time – as if they are having a body language conversational dance, with both parties' movements synchronised.

The smile is critical

Giving someone a genuine warm smile is one of the most important skills for getting into rapport with someone and then developing and maintaining your new relationship.

Irrespective of all other physical features, the one that can make you look more attractive for both males and females is the smile. A smile is recognised in every culture and serves important social functions – inviting friendship, showing deference and even hoping for appeasement.[6]

Research[7] suggests that a smile just cannot be ignored. A good smile is always very attractive to another person. A smile is the only facial expression that can be recognised as far away as 30 metres.

'What sunshine is to flowers so a smile is to humanity.'

Anon

When someone smiles at you it is almost irresistible and you nearly always feel yourself (i.e. it happens before you even realise it) smiling back. It is said that the best thing you can do with your face is smile, and it is so true for almost every social interaction. When we like someone we smile; if we see a smiling face we think automatically that they like us – it is ego boosting to be liked.[8]

brilliant impact

A smile will make you look*:

- More friendly.
- More intelligent.
- More physically attractive.
- More co-operative.
- More reliable.
- More influential.
- More fit.
- More popular.
- More honest.
- More agreeable.
- More emotionally stable.[9]

---

* Obviously not just one smile, and in this list there is considerable overlap and inclusion, but the point holds well.

And in life a smile will give you:

- More job offers.
- A higher salary.
- Perhaps more romantic partners.

And even a lower jail sentence!

'Sometimes your joy is the source of your smile, but sometimes your smile can be the source of your joy.'

Thich Nhat Hanh, Vietnamese, Zen Buddhist monk

One of the reasons why models on the catwalk are either straight-faced or pout is because the designers want you to look at their collections, not be distracted by the beauty of the model. This changes as soon as the model is promoting a product, because there we almost invariably see their very expensive orthodontia.

Interestingly, women smile more than men and will use a half smile to maintain the flow of conversation. Also, women are not as impressed by a smile from men as men are from women, since as they are more efficient at making social evaluations than men,[10] possibly because social interaction with men can have significant consequences.

brilliant tips

1   Women who smile less are adversely rated as less carefree, happy and relaxed, but this is not so in males.

2   Males – if you wish to appear more powerful when in the company of other men, smile less[11].

Types of smile

There are two types of smile and it is very important to know how to perceive and to give the appropriate smile.

Genuine smiles[12] (sometimes called Duchenne) involve the whole face and two specific actions. First the corners of the lips are curled and pulled back and up, then secondly the cheeks are raised, which causes little wrinkles (crow's feet) around the eyes. Both these occur naturally, mainly unconsciously, and act as an indicator of delight. In false smiles (non-Duchenne) it is only the mouth that moves, and these smiles are usually consciously performed and do not show any genuine feelings.

The Chinese have a saying:

'*Never trust a man who smiles only with his mouth.*'

This it is true because a real smile involves the eyes, supported by crinkly crow's feet (although nowadays these are not so frequent in the more mature population – Botox has a lot to answer for!).

In addition to this, whereas the corners of the mouth look the same in a genuine smile, if the person is feeling anxious one or the other side of their mouth tends to drop.

brilliant tip

Make sure that you smile with your whole face so that it is genuine and appears so.

On the left is a classic non-Duchenne smile where only the mouth is moving, making the smile somewhat supercilious. On the right is an example of a Duchenne smile – notice the crow's feet round the eyes, the mouth being pulled back so much that the teeth are revealed and the head slightly dipped.

Rapport, tics and accents

In fact getting into rapport requires more than just your body language; speech patterns such as loudness, and speed of delivery also have an important effect. Additionally, if the person has word tics such as 'You know', 'Actually', 'Basically', 'Like', etc., these too can be used to accelerate rapport when occasionally employed in conversation with someone who has a tic. (See the section on verbal tics on page 180.)

It is said that some sales managers will recruit salespeople who have the same regional accent as those to whom they are selling, because they are able to get into rapport quicker with their prospects than others who do not have the same linguistic facility. (She/he talks like us so she/he must be OK.)

We like people who are most like us and unfortunately this translates into ideas of supposed superiority.[13] Our family/clan/tribe/nation is better than yours is a very common position taken by groups who share the same characteristics.

The handshake

Again, like the clothes we wear, the handshake is not body language in the true sense, in as much as it is a conscious rather than an unconscious act.

Psychologist Dr F. Chaplin researched handshaking and found that there is a high correlation between a good handshake and a positive first impression.[14]

In this study it was also suggested that one's handshake was constant over time and did not change, and that shy people and those who were neurotic gave a softer or more limp handshake. Perhaps we knew that intuitively anyway, but what was also interesting was that it was found that women who were more open and liberal in their views, and/or intellectual, gave a firm handshake and made a more positive first impression. Here is the kicker: men who display the same dispositional characteristics as these women typically gave a somewhat less firm handshake and consequently made a poor first impression – not because their handshake was similar to that of a female, but because men are supposed to have a firmer grip.

'The result of this study differs from the typical finding that women who exhibit confident behavior that is similar to the behavior of men often make a more negative impression than the men … giving a firm handshake may provide an effective initial form of self-promotion for women that does not have the costs associated with other less subtle forms of assertive self-promotion.'

Dr F. Chaplin

So, to state the obvious for this social ritual:

- Stand upright when you meet someone – it makes you look your tallest.
- Stand straight with your shoulders back – for the same reason.
- Establish eye contact – you project confidence.
- Give a full smile – you project friendliness.[15]
- Be the first to extend your hand – it projects personal confidence and power.
- Grip the other person's hand firmly.
- Shake for three seconds only – on first meeting you do not want to appear too friendly.

Other obvious strategies include:

- At social gatherings, keep food and drink in your left hand.
- If you tend to have sweaty hands, run them under cold water before you work the room and, for men, keep a tissue in your right-hand pocket.

Additional tips for handshakes for presidents, political and executive hopefuls and the rest of us are:

1 **Ensure that the palm of your right hand is dry**. When we are anxious we perspire in all sorts of places (see page 66), but especially on the palms of our hands. If you do not want to appear anxious when you first meet someone and indicate non-verbally that you are anxious, then just before the handshake dry your hand on a handkerchief discreetly kept in your right pocket. A hand in the pocket whilst standing tall is a great sign of confidence.

2 **Initiate the handshake**. Always initiate the handshake as it shows you are taking the lead, are more confident and also it provides you with an opportunity to play the

following four games which will, as the Americans say, make you look like 'a winner'.

3   **Achieve the top/prone with your right hand**. You can play the 'top-hand turn' game – as you grip the other person's hand, turn it to your left so that the back of your hand is uppermost – it shows that you are the more dominant person. If the other party does not allow you to play this game and keeps your hand vertical, you can play the 'left-hand top' game. As you shake hands your left hand is placed over the 'shake' showing that you are still the more dominant.

4   **Move the handshake into their personal zone**. As you shake hands push your arm forward so that the handshake is in the other person's personal zone, so that they appear to be conceding to you more space (see proxemics on page 28). You appear the stronger of the two as well as the more dominant. In photographs, too, more of your arm is shown.

5   **Maximise contact with your left hand**. Do the 'bicep shuffle' at every photo opportunity when meeting powerful dignities. As you shake hands, grasp the person's bicep gently – but beware this can look silly, especially when both parties try to do it at the same time in an attempt to show who is the most powerful, confident or dominant. (Politicians: do not do this to a royal otherwise your political ratings will fall by at least ten points!)

6   **Position yourself for official photographs**. Always stand to your dignitary's right so that when you do the 'bicep shuffle' more of your right arm is shown, which means you appear to dominate the photo that appears in the press the next day.

7   **Special tip for females**. Chauvinist males will often try

and play some or all of the handshake games above. Also, for obvious inappropriate reasons, they may attempt to prolong the physical contact. Here is the strategy for dealing with these males:

- Keep your elbow locked as much as you can in a right angle.
- Push the man's hand as hard as you can to his side of the personal zone. It will be easier than you think because he will not be expecting it and his elbow will not be locked.
- Play games 1–3 above.
- Look the man in the eyes briefly and do not smile.

8 **Handshake tips for female royals:**

- Keep your gloves on – it reminds the other person of your aristocratic heritage.
- Sit down if you want to, since it is usually more comfortable; in your position you do not need to make a favourable impression and you are a smaller target, which will please your security people. It is said that Queen Victoria would always sit as much as possible, perhaps because she had a medical condition, but if you sit and everyone else has to stand, who looks the more important?

9 **Photo opportunities**. If there is going to be a photo opportunity and you are sitting with three dignitaries you can show how you are more aligned with the interests of one of them by moving your chair closer to your ally.

Advanced rapport skills

Let's move on from the handshake games of the powerful and famous to the more practical aspects of getting into rapport and maintaining it. If you find this section interesting, I suggest you invest in the sister book to this title, *Brilliant NLP.*[16]

Mirroring

Mirroring will test your credibility. Mirroring occurs naturally and we all do it without any training whatsoever, especially with people with whom we are friendly. Mirroring is presenting a 'mirror image' of the other person – if you move they move, if you lean forward they lean forward, if you smile they smile, if you nod your head they nod their head, etc. For each of us it is incredibly difficult not to do this as, interestingly, even before we were born, the rate of our heartbeat matched that of our mother's when both of us were relaxed.

Mirroring is certainly effective when you want to get into rapport with someone. It is essential to practise if you wish to develop this skill. (See activities on page 203.) With continual practice you will be able to mirror without even thinking – you already mirror naturally with friends, but you should not attempt to mirror with strangers until it is naturally part of you, otherwise you will never get into rapport. Nobody likes to be mimicked.

A couple mirroring each other. See if you can identify five signs here that provide a mirroring cluster. If the male is leading, what is his next body movement? If the female is leading, what will be her next likely movement? Answers on page 223.

Pacing

Pacing is mirroring part two. Pacing is the bridge between two people that is established by mirroring the other person and by sharing things in common – background, friends, interests, experience, etc. By ensuring that you are in the same 'place' as the other person you are constructing the psychological bridge between you which is essential for rapport. It is helpful to check that you have achieved rapport with the person you are with; you can do this by consciously deciding to move in a certain way. For instance, if you are sitting and talking, when you wish to emphasise something move forward a little. If the other person also moves forward at the same time or very soon after then you know that you have established rapport. If they do not move in sync with you then you know that you have not established rapport. So continue leading with small changes in your body language for a little while longer and try again until you achieve success with reciprocal mirroring. This is called 'leading', since you have to lead the person's body language.

To check if you are in full rapport with someone:

Mirror ⟶ Pace ⟶ Lead ⟶ Rapport

If the person does not follow your lead then repeat the process. If after four attempts you are not successful, try a different approach in what you are saying or doing. Sometimes duplicating their 'tic' – either physical or verbal – assists in achieving rapport. If the tic is very overt it would not be appropriate to mirror and could be highly embarrassing to the person, so in such a case just move your thumb slightly each time the tic occurs.

If you are still not successful do not be hard on yourself; for a whole host of reasons some people will just not like us. Even professional psychologists are not successful every time.

Having achieved rapport we might wish to ooze confidence, so this comes next.

> **brilliant** recap
>
> - Give genuine (Duchenne) smiles often.
> - Stand tall.
> - Initiate a firm handshake.
> - Speak at the same rate as the other person.
> - If the other person has a verbal tic, use it sparingly.
> - Develop mirroring skills and then use them.
> - Develop pacing skills and then use them.

References

[1] Lakin, J. (2003), 'The chameleon effect as social glue', *Journal of Nonverbal Behaviour* 27.

[2] O'Connor, J. and Seymour, J. (1990), *Introducing Neuro-Linguistic Programming*.

[3] Keating, C. F. (2006), 'Functional approaches to nonverbal impression management', *The Sage Handbook of Nonverbal Communication*.

[4] Krumhuber, E. and Manstead, A. S. R. (2007), 'The effects of smile dynamics, head tilt and gender', *Journal of Nonverbal Behaviour* 39.

[5] Bandler, R. and Grinder, J. (1975), *The Structure of Magic I: A Book about Language and Therapy*, and *The Structure of Magic II: A Book about Communication and Change*.

[6] Henley, N. M. (1977), *Body Politics: Power, sex and nonverbal communication*.

[7] Cunningham, M. R. et al. (1990), 'What do women want?' *Journal of Personality and Social Psychology* 59.

[8] Higgins, E. T. (1987), 'Self-discrepancy: a theory relating self and affect', *Psychological Review* 94.

[9] Mehu, M. et al. (2008), 'Sex differences in the effect of smiling on social judgements', *Journal of Social, Evolutionary and Cultural Psychology* 2.

[10] Hall, J. A. and Matsmoto, D. (2004), 'Gender differences in judgements of multiple emotions from facial expressions', *Emotions* 4.

[11] Keating, C. F. (1985), 'Body politics, human dominance signals, the primate in us', in S. L. Ellyson and J. F. Dovidio, *Power, Dominance and Non-verbal Behaviour.*

[12] Ekman, P. et al. (1980), 'Facial signs of emotional agreement', *Journal of Personality and Social Psychology* 39.

[13] To appreciate how powerful this is you might like to read up on Jane Elliot's frightening exercise – Blue Eyes/Brown Eyes – of the 1960s, and the Stanford prison experiment in 1971.

[14] Chaplin, W. F. et al. (2000), 'Handshaking, gender, personality and first impressions', *Journal of Personality and Social Psychology* 79.

[15] *Ibid.*

[16] Molden, D. and Hutchinson, P. (2006), *Brilliant NLP.*

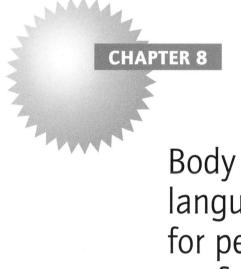

CHAPTER 8

Body language for personal confidence

Confidence is what confidence does

Confidence is a major key to success in life. Having confidence encourages you to take calculated risks and seize the opportunities that life presents. Confidence is what Rosabeth Moss Kanter, the Harvard guru, called, 'that sweet spot between arrogance and despair'. However, it is essential to have confidence in yourself before you can undertake most activities.

Anxiety acts like a downward spiral on confidence. Of course, some of us are naturally more anxious than others because we have that psychological trait, but for most it is brought about by what is occurring in our environment, and this is called state or context anxiety. Either way, with some conscious changes in our body language we can mask this emotion so that we actually appear to be confident.

When we are anxious our body language reverts to the tricks and strategies we found effective so many millions of years ago. When we are faced with a difficult or stressful situation we indulge in the three Fs – that is, fight, flight or freeze – and our bodies prepare us for each of these contingencies.

Perhaps confidence is shown most in the fight response, where we don our psychological armour by standing tall, tensing our muscles, square on to the 'enemy', engaging in high eye contact, making a fist with our hands and clenching our jaw. Here we are doing our best to appear confident irrespective of what our internal feelings may be. Aggression creates aggression so this is not recommended.

brilliant definition

Confidence (noun)

Feeling and knowing that one has the necessary competencies and skills to manage an interpersonal event.

Unfortunately, loss of confidence and a preparedness to flee or freeze has numerous way of seeping through our body language. It is important to look for clusters of body changes rather than build a conclusion on just one or two signs, and so therefore it is best if we can control at least some of the changes/responses in our bodies.

Breathe slowly

One of the classic ways of reducing physical stress is to breathe slowly and deeply using your tummy and diaphragm rather than your chest muscles. (See breathing in threes on page 72.) When an individual goes into a fight or flight mode, because they are threatened they breathe more quickly to take in more oxygen. People who are confident of their ability to manage a situation do not need to fight or run away so they breathe normally. Whilst our breathing speed increases without our knowing, you soon become aware of it. So, unless the situation deserves it, and most situations do not, to appear confident you need to deliberately control and slow down your breathing.

If your body is screaming to flight or fight the slow breathing will be the equivalent of your body saying to your brain 'everything is OK here – just calm down'. This is because there is a complex reciprocal relationship between the body and the mind. Just watch seasoned politicians when they are being challenged on television by experienced journalists; they show signs of anxiety in other ways when they are being pressured, but increased breathing rate is not usually one of them.

When someone is anxious they naturally tighten their muscles to protect their body. Take a moment to attempt to tighten your chest and tummy muscles and breathe slowly with your tummy and diaphragm at the same time – it is very difficult, if not impossible.

So breathe slowly.

Make eye contact

When we are intimidated, a sign of lacking in confidence is that we look away.*

In looking away we are looking for options of escape from the person or situation. Boxers at their weigh-in before the big fight attempt to 'stare down' their opponent in an attempt to gain a psychological advantage which they hope will give them a subsequent physical advantage in the boxing ring later.

Not that we are advocating staring down everyone that you meet, but certainly in making normal eye contact you will appear more confident.

(See the chapter on assertiveness for more discussion on eye contact – pages 107–17.)

Your smile

We have already spoken about the smile at great length (see page 79). It is a fact that we can only give a full (Duchenne)

---

* Interestingly, not making eye contact when giving instructions can be interpreted as a sign of power.

smile when we are relaxed and confident; however, do not smile continually, as a 'genuine' smile is difficult to fake for any length of time. If your eyes stop smiling your mouth smile will be interpreted as anxiety. If you smile too much you will look as if you're trying to 'people please' or submit to the person. The confident person smiles when they wish to; they do not need the approval of others.

Stand tall

Height in humans is always better;[1] taller people are thought to be more positive, secure, masculine, successful, capable, confident, etc. Taller men certainly earn more than their shorter brothers[2] (see opposite).

Toads, puffer fish, lizards and chameleons, when they wish to impress and pretend that they are not really frightened, all make themselves much bigger. We are not much different when we want to appear more confident.

Probably ever since *Homo sapiens* walked out of Africa, mothers have been telling their children to stand up and stand straight. Mothers intuitively know lots of things, one of which is that height is strongly associated with power and communicates an attitude of confidence. Most children are told to eat their veggies so that they will be 'tall and strong'. Relations tell little boys, 'My, how tall you are'. Our society is obsessed with male height, with an unjustified cultural mindset thinking that somehow to be tall gives one all these advantageous traits. Squadies are 'square bashed' by their Sergeant Major until they can walk tall. The British Bobby wears a funny dome-shaped cardboard hat to increase the impression of height. In sporting competitions we place the three best athletes on a triple-level podium with the winner standing on the highest step.

Even in religion height is power; the Egyptian and Aztec kings descended from the sun and Zeus and Apollo from Mount

Olympus. Christianity asserts that Jesus came down from heaven and that he ascended (i.e. went back up) into heaven.

Many a height-challenged executive has found that walking tall is a useful strategy, for although they might be smaller than average they appear to be 'psychologically' taller and thus more confident.

It is well established that taller people have better promotion prospects and better pay. Timothy Judge, a business professor at the University of Florida, calculated that for every inch above average height you could add $789 (2003 figures) in additional remuneration each year.[3] This was particularly so in management and sales as opposed to the less 'social' professions such as engineering and accounting. It could be thought that being tall increased one's self-confidence which, of course, had a direct effect on one's performance and which in turn leads to promotions.

Even evolutionary psychologists suggest this might be hardwired into our primitive psyche. As Professor Judge writes:

'They ascribe leader-like qualities to tall people because they (early Homo sapiens) *thought they would be better able to protect themselves and others.'*[4]

It can even be predicted at birth! Boy babies, so a Finnish study in 2005 reports, who were taller than average on their first birthday earned more than their shorter compatriots 50 years later. Taller people are even thought to have a higher intelligence.[5]

Women, too, are in on the look-tall act. Cynthia McKay, when she was the CEO of two multimillion-dollar companies overseeing 510 domestic and international franchises in the USA, wore 3-inch heels, and one would have thought at a natural 5 feet 9 inches in bare feet she was already tall enough! Cynthia McKay's comment, when admitting that she wears heels even though she finds it ridiculous that 3 inches could add to any-one's credibility, stated:

'It is a lot of bunk but it works.'

What has this to do with personal influence? Well, height is power. If you wish to exude power and authority then make yourself as tall as you can, extend your spine, extend your neck so that your head comes up and couple this with putting your shoulders back and down so that they are not hunched – and females should maybe even wear heels.

Sensibly, the designers of the original policeman's hat con-structed it so that the helmet was slightly pointed over the nose. This ensured that to see properly the old-fashioned Bobby had to ensure his head was slightly lifted. Also, the top of the helmet was domed to give the impression of greater height.

So, in body language terms what does this give you? It makes you look confident because metaphorically you appear 'head and shoulders above the rest'. Take it as a fact that the male and female Napoleons amongst us are few and far between and even if you enjoy a Napoleonesque stature the message is the same: walk tall.

Stand still

When you are calm there is very low activity of neurons in your brain's *locus coeruleus*, but we all know and actually feel that when we are anxious, almost the opposite of confidence, our bodies put us into flight or fight mode. We become more attentive and alert. We get an epinephrine and a norepinephrine hit and the catecholamine hormones prepare our muscles for action. Most mammals, including ourselves, start to move either to protect ourselves or to be aggressive. Now, there are some animals that when faced with a threat stand still (because the eye is then better at detecting movement). Consequently, we would do well to follow their example if we wished to appear confident.

Shoulders

When you face someone with confidence your shoulders should be parallel to the person to whom you are speaking. It would be ridiculous to square up to someone and have the lower half of your body showing it was 'ready for the off!' By squaring up to the person it is almost as if you are saying, 'We are equals'.

Also, when your shoulders are parallel with another person you look bigger and thus more confident. Perhaps this explains the use of epaulettes on the shoulders of Mexican generals. (The average height of the American male outranks Mexican males by 3 inches.)

So, square your shoulders.

Chin up

By lifting your chin you automatically lift your eyes, and when you lift your eyes you cannot help but look down, inferring 'I am more superior and thus more confident than you'. If you wish to infer the opposite, you bow your head as well as look down. In some Eastern countries, such as Japan, this action has made it into the realms of social etiquette.

It is said that as soon as the children of the royal house of Hapsburg could walk they had a sprig of holly tied under their neck, so by the time they reached puberty it was natural for them to have a permanently raised chin.

You have probably noticed that when people are depressed they look down, the chin leading the way. These postures have moved into everyday language: 'You look pretty up today' and 'I am feeling down'. It is difficult to appear confident when 'feeling down'.

Sit tall

The same advantage accrues to you when you sit tall. Sitting has an equalising effect, since most of our height comes from our legs. Edward I, who was exceptionally tall, was not only known as the Hammer of the Welsh but also was nicknamed 'Long Shanks'. If height is all in the legs then sitting down certainly has an equalling effect. Have you noticed on chat shows that the host usually looks taller than their guests? This is because their chair is higher and thus gives them a natural air of authority. Many senior executives use the same ploy by ensuring that their chair is higher than those on the other side of their desk.

Talking of work, should you wish to make a point during a meeting you can do two things: sit as tall as you can, and move forward into the 'space' of the meeting. (Refer back to the section on proxemics on page 28.)

Sit still

Watch the Speaker in the House of Commons. He is in control of hundreds of people, not known for their timidity and yet he hardly moves; he is confident, he is in control. Watch powerful captains of industry or cabinet ministers when they appear on TV chat shows and compare them to other celebrities and star-lets. The difference is that the former, being confident, sit very still, as they do not have to perform for the public in order to maintain their status.

Keep your hands still

We use our hands to protect or comfort ourselves (see page 72), so moving our hands more rapidly is a real giveaway, indicating that there is something in the situation that is placing pressure on us or with which we are trying to cope. If we are attacked or challenged verbally, say when we are making a presentation or at an interview, we naturally move our hands to protect ourselves. If during a meeting we are being ignored when making a point, our hand signalling may become more extreme, as if we are saying to our colleagues, 'Hey, it's me, I'm talking, listen to me!'. Watch newscasters on television, they hardly move their hands – why? Because they know that the majority of viewers are listening and watching.

One way to ensure that your hands stay where they should is to 'steeple' them – that is to interlock your fingers and keep your hands on your lap. If you are at a meeting your hands can rest gently on the table. (More of this on pages 206–7.)

Walk slowly

Just think about it – have you ever seen a senior politician of any nationality run? (With the exception of American Presidents who like to run up the stairs of Air Force One to show how fit they are.)

When you run you are telling the world that someone more important than yourself will be kept waiting and that you are but a mere minion. Of course, sometimes we have to run, as Chaucer reminds us in his *Clerk's Tale*: 'time and tide wait for no man' (or 'Ay fleeth the tyme, it nil no man abyde'), but if we want to appear confident then we must practise better time management!

'In Hollywood powerful people speak fast and walk slow.'

Michael Caine

Drink more water

As we know from watching cartoons there is a tendency in most of us to swallow more when we are under stress, or we clear our throat before we speak. This is because our throat tightens with anxiety; the net result being that we appear lacking in confidence. The solution is quite easy: always have a glass of water available. If you are challenged, make yourself appear confident by making people wait for an answer by taking a sip before you respond.

Speak slowly

When we are anxious there is a tendency to speak quickly in order to get what we have to say over and done with, perhaps because we are concerned that people will not bother to listen or are too busy. What is the right speed? Listen to newscasters both on radio and television. Speaking slowly will also assist in the comprehension of your listeners and, contrary to what you would expect, it is more persuasive.[6]

No wonder John Wayne always sounded confident; not unlike Margaret Thatcher, on many occasions he took a breath in the middle of a sentence. Mrs Thatcher, it is said, employed this tactic so that the interviewer could not interrupt her, ensuring she had enough air not to need to breathe as she launched into her next sentence.

Remember the actor John Wayne (aka for fans of old Westerns, 'The Duke')? When challenged as to why he took breaths in this way whilst he spoke, he is reputed to have said, slowly, of course:

'Just to let them know ... [deep breath] ... I ain't done yet.'

brilliant recap

● So, look confident, breathe slowly.

● So, look confident, look them in the eye.

● So, look confident, smile.

● So, look confident, stand tall.

● So, look confident, stand still.

● So, look confident, chin up.

● So, look confident, sit tall.

● So, look confident, keep your hands still.

● So, look confident, walk slowly.

● So, look more confident, drink more water.

● So, look more confident, speak slowly.

References

[1] Judge, T. A. and Cable, D. M. (2004), 'The effect of physical height on workplace success and income: preliminary test of a theoretical model', *Journal of Applied Psychology* 89.

[2] 'Short guys finish last', *The Economist*, 23 December 1995.

[3] Judge, T. et al. (2004), 'The forgotten ones?: The validity of consideration and initiating structure in leadership research', *Journal of Applied Psychology* 89.

[4] *Ibid.*

[5] Hall, T. (1982), *The Hidden Dimension.*

[6] Jones, C., Berry, L. and Stevens, C. (2007), 'Synthesized speech intelligibility and persuasion: Speech rate and non-native listeners', *Computer Speech and Language* 21: 641–651.

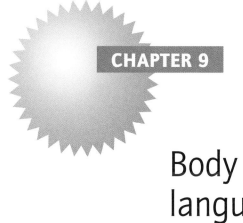

CHAPTER 9

Body language for assertiveness

'Standing up' for yourself

In being assertive the basic principle is to make yourself as visible as possible. By the way they hold themselves people gives away a tremendous amount of information about themselves which can even include an indication of their disposition.

If you are going to be assertive you have to look calm, confident and deliberate. If you have difficulties doing this, remember that no one can see how anxious you are inside your head. Yes, there is seepage of the truth in one's body language, but the good news is that we can practise control and practise makes perfect. In private moments you can be like the actor instructed by the director to repeat take after take until the scene is perfect.

brilliant definition

Assertive (adjective)

Being bold and confident in your demeanour and being able to insist on what you need by expressing yourself emphatically whilst being calm and retaining self-control.

Here are some 'acting' instructions for assertiveness:

Stand tall

Demographic changes in Britain identified the need to recruit people from a range of ethnic groups, but there was a 'tall' matter to be resolved: you could not become a policeman unless you were over a certain height and so the requirement was modified. Height has always and universally indicated power (see page 98) and authority. Without being rude to those of us who are height-challenged, one could imagine that it be might be difficult for a 4 foot 8 inch teacher to be assertive with a 6 foot teenager who was doing what some teenagers do with spray cans and pristine school walls. Even so, standing as tall as they could would be helpful.

Powerful people are even thought to be taller. Napoleon was either 5 foot 2 or 5, depending whether you support the English or French findings, but, so it is said, he was thought by his countrymen at the time to be at least 6 foot. 'Le petit corporal' was just good English propaganda.

Women wishing to make themselves appear taller will toss or flick their hair. For some men, height in women is an advantage. Take Tom Cruise; with Nicole Kidman being 4 inches taller and Katie Holmes 3 inches above him … but I digress.

When being introduced to a dignitary or royalty, men bow and ladies curtsey, making themselves smaller than they are and thus recognising the superiority/power of the other person. So, when being assertive it is helpful to give the impression of as much superiority and power as possible.

Now you know why when being stopped by the police one of the officers will make their way to your car quite quickly, so that they are standing way above you as you sit in your car seat. They have a double assertive advantage: you cannot move, and you have to look up to make eye contact with the officer.

So, if you want to be assertive – stand tall.

Stand wide

With your shoulders hunched and your body and feet heading for the door you will look more like the victim. So, using body language to appear assertive means displaying as much of yourself as possible; this is sometimes called the 'peacock factor', because the male peacock's tail when displayed demands a huge amount of space.

Two sportsmen making themselves as wide as possible. The athlete on the left is using his hands to push his arms forward as well as to show off his biceps; the one on the right creates the same effect by having his arms akimbo.

Point your feet towards the person with whom you are interacting and be 'at ease', that is, with feet slightly apart. Soldiers stand to attention when commanded to by their superior officer – this might look good on the parade ground but it is definitely not the look of an assertive person.

Face up

Imagine that you have a Post-it® note on the end your nose! Now, keep it at right angles to the ground so that you are neither jutting your head forward, showing aggression, or leaning back attempting to avoid an imaginary uppercut to the chin, suggesting arrogance. Looking down your nose at someone is not likely to get the other person on side.

There are exceptions to this when you want to move from being assertive to being dominant, and here we are back to proxemics. We spoke of policemen earlier, and in some constabularies if an officer is having difficulty in gaining compliance they learn as part of their training to deliberately move into the individual's personal zone. If the officer has the height advantage they can look down on the non-cooperative person using dominance as a way of gaining interpersonal control.

Eyes straight

Eye contact needs to be established without staring or glaring, which is aggressive and threatening to the other person. Eye contact has the effect of looking more dominant.[1] When you look away, do your best not to look down, which is a sign of submission. Also, looking down with our eyes, so those who are expert in NLP tell us, indicates that we are accessing feelings. In being assertive we want to be as logical as possible and not be making emotional appeals or statements, although this is not to do with body language.

Interestingly, if you have brown eyes you are thought to be more dominant and thus assertive.[2]

Arms down

As we have noted, one of the signs of being confident is to have open gestures. It is very sensible to raise our arms above our waist to defend ourselves when under attack or when we are frightened. This natural response spills over when we are in the presence of a dominant person or when we are facing a difficult situation. If we wish to be assertive, or confident for that matter, we need to drop our arms, thus showing that we are so confident that we can offer and display the more vulnerable parts of our bodies. Maybe you have seen film clips of how that great world champion boxer Muhammad Ali would taunt his adversaries in the ring by keeping his arms down whilst he danced around the ring? He was saying to his opponents the equivalent of: 'I am not frightened of you because I am so good that you cannot hurt me'. He was not being aggressive, he was not being passive, just confident in his own pugilistic skills and thus assertive.

Hands

We greet and say goodbye to colleagues by the strange ritual of shaking hands; this is now almost the universal gesture to assure the other person that we have no weapon, nor is our fist clenched to strike.

Body builders pronate their arms so that the back of their hands face forward, which moves the elbows outwards. This shows off their muscled shoulders and big biceps so that they look stronger and bigger.

We also have a tendency to grip things when we are nervous or frightened. We hang on for comfort; a reflex action we used as very young children, hanging on to our mothers when we were fearful.

Hand movements have been classified as either 'proximal' or 'distal'. The former is when your hands are directed towards yourself, such as placing a hand over your mouth or hugging yourself; these are usually signs of self-doubt, anxiety or fear. Distal is when the hands are directed away from one's body; this is a friendship sign, such as waving to someone or holding out your arms to welcome or hug someone. Many religious statues adopt this pose: Jesus for Christians, Buddha for Buddhists and Ganesha for Hindus (Confucius is the exception).

Typical religious statues showing distal hand signs.

Putting this all together, to be assertive our hands need to be open, not pronated, and should not be seen to be gripping something.

Physical distance

We said much about this before (see page 26), but here it is only important to remember that when being assertive you ensure that your distance from the other person should be in the appropriate zone; about the same distance you would maintain with a colleague in normal public conversation. Obviously you do not want to be invading their personal space, which is aggressive, nor be so far away as to look as if you are ready to run. So how far is preferable? Just over an arm's length is about the norm in Western cultures; their waist should be just on your peripheral vision as you make eye contact.

However, if you are not being successful, say when you want to make a definite point, then move slightly into the other person's space. Is this aggressive? Yes, it is, but when you want something done managers learn early that there are no prizes for being Mr or Ms Nice Person with difficult or lazy employees. Points are first won for results – the iron fist within the …

Voice, use of the assumptive and those transitive verbs

Obviously a calm voice delivered slowly in a paced and measured manner is going to be more successful than one which is loudly aggressive and intimidating, or the opposite – unnecessarily soft, timid or high pitched. Instructions given quickly or hesitantly can give the impression of nervousness or anxiety, and the words employed should be short, specific and behavioural.

In Australia there is a verbal style that has an upward inflection at the end of a statement. It is as if everyone is asking one another questions. If this is used in the UK it is taken as a question and not only does it sound weak and passive but it leaves the other person with the initiative, thinking 'Shall I?' or 'Won't I?'

When issuing an instruction in an assertive way there is a huge difference between 'I would like you to … please' and 'I would like you to … thank you'. The first example is good management, but if you need to be assertive the latter with the 'thank you' is assumptive because it assumes that what is requested will be done. It subtly changes your request into an order.

brilliant tip

To be assertive when you ask for something, always say 'thank you' and not 'please'.

Baton gestures

When being assertive there is a danger of using what are known as 'baton gestures' with one's arms. This is when they are used to highlight or punctuate our speech, especially when we want to emphasise a point; it's great for public speaking and addresses but not in one-to-one situations.

Baton gestures include such arm movements as aggressive pointing or wagging a finger in someone's face or, as some politicians do when they want to appear confident and assertive, karate chops in the air. This display of forcefulness usually has the reverse effect: aggression is met with counter-aggression.

Confident we may be, but can we make ourselves attractive? Read on …

brilliant recap

- Stand tall.
- Stand wide.
- Keep your shoulders parallel.
- Hold your head up.
- Maintain eye contact.
- Do not move back.

References

[1] Burgoon, J. K. et al. (1996), *Non-verbal Communication: The Unspoken Dialogue*.

[2] Kleisner, K. et al. (2010), 'Eye colour predicts but does not directly influence perceived dominance in men', *Personality and Individual Differences* 49 (1): 59–64.

CHAPTER 10

Body language and attraction

Making the most of what you've got

Before you delve into this chapter I have to make an apology: there is a lot about sex here and because it underlies so much, if not drives the body language of attraction, there is much repetition but from different perspectives.

What women like and need and what men like and need is addressed again and again because, let's just say it and get it over with, most males are programmed to be promiscuous; most females are programmed (some would say sentenced) to be selective. Males seek primarily physical satisfaction; females desire social satisfaction. Women choose their men; men compete to be chosen. Males produce millions of sperm; females have a limited number of eggs. Both choose the best partnering option they can for the production of offspring; males by having as many children as possible, females by having as many as can be nurtured to adulthood.

brilliant definition

Attraction (noun)

The facility to manifest qualities such as interest, charm, fascination, amusement and generosity such that others seek your company.

Let's get real, too. Men do not, as Dr Alfred Kinsey[1] suggested, think about sex every 7 seconds. It is only several times a day, according to the US National Academy of Scientists, and it is only slightly lower for women.

Nevertheless, it is not money that makes the world go round but that very basic need we call sex. This is where the language of words literally loses 'hands down' to body language. In the early part of relationships body shape and what we do with it really does speak louder than words.[2]

As most women will attest, it is an unfair and inappropriate world. Basically, fertility is written all over the female body. For women the quadriga of youth, bust, hair and body shape dominate the way a woman is initially viewed or valued by the male and, to a certain extent, by society.*

---

brilliant example

One of the reasons Alan Ayckbourn[3] felt so moved to write his insightful play *Body Language* was because, as a writer when checking the top book rankings in the Sunday papers, it suddenly dawned on him:

'The English best-seller books in any week usually consist of four books about dieting, six books about make-up and so on. So, we are indeed an obsessive nation.'

With the advent of feminism in the 1960s one might have expected that such discrimination would have waned, but 'lookism' does prevail[4] and unlike gender, sexual orientation, race, religion and political orientation, or country of origin, it

---

* It was only 300 years ago that Addison wrote that it was unjust to treat old and feeble women as witches and the persecution of witches only became illegal in Britain in 1735. Buss, David (2003) *The Evolution of Desire.*

would almost be impossible to legislate against this because it is so individual.

Our sexuality is unique among mammals. Sex for other mammals is driven primarily by their biology and for the most part it is an instinctive approach. We still have our instincts, we still have the same physiology, but now there is a very thin veneer of our cultural heritage and social mores. Most animals have sex when they are ready; we humans have sex dancing through the requirements of our cultural heritage and our psychological hurdles.

No wonder it is complicated, as Dr Alfred Kinsey over 60 years ago suggested:

'... sex is dealt with in the current confusion of ignorance and sophistication, denial and indulgence, suppression and stimulation, punishment and exploitation, secrecy and display.' [5]

Here, what is of interest to both sexes are the secondary sexual characteristics. Unless you are a young performing pop star of either sex they are not usually accentuated. Most of the body language of attraction then is how we accentuate and articulate our secondary characteristics.

Note: In this section, perhaps more than the others, we are talking in generalities and there are always exceptions to the rules of attractiveness.

Primacy and recency

An additional point on first male/female impressions we must cover is what is known as the 'primacy' and 'recency' effects; that is, the first and last things that we see and hear when we meet someone for the first time. We have covered at length how important first impressions are (primacy effect) but the recency effect is almost, but not quite, as powerful.

To illustrate this, read out to a friend the same string of numbers (6140903602786) three times slowly and then ask them to write down as many as they can remember. Most will remember 6140 and 2786 – i.e. the first and the last.

What happens here is that our short-term memory when we first hear the string of numbers kicks in so they are easily remembered and there is time for rehearsal. The recency effect is similar when recalling the numbers from short-term memory.

Now let's put this psych stuff into what happens when you meet someone that you are interested in for the first time, especially if you find them attractive.

We can express this graphically:

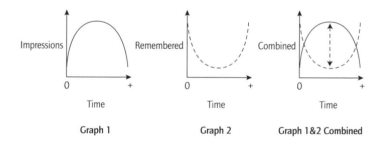

| Graph 1 | Graph 2 | Graph 1&2 Combined |

Graph 1 suggests that you are slightly anxious to make a great impression on the person. You begin somewhat nervously but grow in confidence. Then, say, about halfway through you have difficulty maintaining your most alluring and attractive self (male or female); your nervousness returns and your 'performance' drops.

Graph 2 shows the effect of primacy and recency in the person to whom you are attracted. They remember your first and last impression.

Graph 3 combines Graphs 1 and 2. Unfortunately, as you can see, when you were at your most sparkly your behaviour is not being registered as significantly as that at the start and end of the encounter.

brilliant tip

When you plan to meet or introduce yourself for the first time, make sure that not only do you plan your 'approach' but also your 'retreat' to ensure you have created the best first and last impression that you can.

First we will cover briefly those things that we cannot do much about, mainly because we recruited the wrong grandparents. Here we are reflecting on the bodies we were blessed with unless, of course, we indulge in artificial help – and many of us do!

Unfortunately for the political correctness and equality brigade, looks do count. Research paper after research paper shout from the academic journals that 'beauty is best/better/good/significant/successful'.

Those not so blessed have, in the past, blamed this obsession with looks on the media – who constantly bombard us with photo after picture after photo of the fortunate 5 per cent of the population that fall into this category. Not so, says research. 'If the world were to eliminate every magazine and media form containing images of youthful, flawless bodies, we would still create and desire these images in our minds', says Harvard psychologist Nancy Etcoff.[6] We are the descendents of those who chose physical beauty.

So, if we are to believe the evolutionary psychologists, we have to face facts: beauty/handsomeness is better.[7] Those who were given the beauty pills at birth enjoy a much better life than the rest of us. You fly in the face of reality if you do not accept that society is seduced by attractiveness. Beautiful people invite more interpersonal attention – whether male or female. If you want to surprise an exceptionally attractive person, ignore them and flirt with their friend; as they expect to be the centre of interpersonal attention or admiration,[8] their response is interesting.

Should you have done something inappropriate at work or socially, the more attractive you are the less blame is attributed to you.[9] If you have been criminal, you might get a lower prison sentence.[10]

Enough. Enough about things that 95 per cent of us cannot do anything about and let's move on to things we can.

Propinquity

In psychology, propinquity is a very old concept going back to the 1930s[11] and, like most of social psychology, once you have thought it through it is obvious. Simply stated, the more time we spend with another the more they are likely to like us and we them.

In industry there is now a movement called 'The Allen Curve'[12] – this is that rather than having people in separate offices, they work in a large open-plan space. Propinquity is at work here, too, because the employees talk to each other rather than use technology to communicate, and performance is improved. There are variations on the phrase but they all demonstrate propinquity: 'Married couples that dine/pray/garden together, stay together'.

So, if you want to be liked, employ a little propinquity and just let the conversation happen and the relationship might bloom. This old adage just might be true:

'Time equals commitment.'

Endogamy

For most of our history as humans there have been strict rules about who you could and could not marry. Although the restrictive and discriminatory laws may be gone, we still tend to like people like ourselves in terms of colour, religion, culture, social standing – right down to the way we dress and even eye colour.

So, if you want to be liked and found attractive, be as like as you possibly can to your target group or the person with whom you are smitten.

Even Cicero 100 years before Christ wrote:

'Like readily consorts with like.'

In 1967 the ban of a mixed marriage between a Caucasian and an African American was ruled unconstitutional in 16 states in the USA. We all owe a huge debt to Martin Luther King.

Stay around attractive people.

What we can do is cultivate friendships with attractive people. Patronage has a long history and is alive and well today. The same principle operates in attractiveness; an unattractive man who has an attractive wife is viewed as more attractive, and vice versa. Individuals themselves feel more attractive if they have an attractive partner.

Height

We have spoken of the advantages of height for men elsewhere (see page 98). It is well known in the attractiveness stakes that women prefer men who are taller than average and taller than themselves. Perhaps this goes back to their ancestral pre-occupation of desiring a caveman protector for herself and her

offspring. Men, not surprisingly, much prefer their female partners to be shorter than themselves.[13] Imagine how Ms De-Fen
Yao from China feels being the tallest living women in the world,
standing at 7 foot 9 inches (2.3m).[14]

If you are height challenged you know that there are other
factors that add to one's attractiveness, such as personality,
interpersonal skills and power. Also, usually you place more
effort in the development of these alternative fundamentals.

Hair

For women, strong lustrous hair[15] is an indicator of youth, thus
explaining all those neotenic models pouting out of adverts of
coiffeur salons all over the world promoting hair products. Youth,
again, is one of the reasons it is said that men prefer blondes, as
it is less common to be a natural blonde after a woman reaches
30 years of age.[16] With the perennial march of time, blonde hair
becomes darker.

Bad hair and skin during medieval times were signs of sickness
and this is endorsed by today's medical standards, as poor hair
and hair loss can be an indication of iron deficiency caused by
blood loss, diabetes, thyroid disease and malnutrition.

Male baldness is not found attractive by some women, particularly younger women.[17] However, if you are follically challenged
in the upper follicle department, just call to mind Bruce Willis,
Dr Phil, Sean Connery and … Homer Simpson (I joke!).

Body shape

With body shape let us state and start with the obvious.

Most men like those physical attributes that give an indication of
positive sexual reproduction – breasts, legs, bottoms, hourglass
figure and that major sign of youth, a good skin. Women on the

other hand, put far less emphasis on the procreative and more on the protective. For many women strong upright shoulders, a strong chin, muscled arms, a trim bottom and strong legs are gazed upon with pleasure, especially when it is topped off with a V-shaped torso. For most of us males it gets worse, since the research suggests[18] a waist to shoulder ratio of 0.75 is the most attractive. That is why so many men spend hours in the gym trying to make their normal manly bodies more manly and hiding their non-exercised legs, which now, compared to their muscled upper bodies, appear relatively skinny. Perhaps males should thank Beau Brummell for making long trousers fashionable.

There is some suggestion that young men prefer a slimmer female, and as they grow older, some would say more sensible, preference increases for what we might call the more generous, or in the adjective of the singles adverts, 'cuddly' frame.

Unfortunately for the obese they are not regarded as physically attractive. Even children[19] as young as six years old impute the unfavourable attributes to them. Here the implications impact not only on relationships but also employment.

Also stating the obvious, because it is usually only young to lower middle-age females that can reproduce easily, men have a preference for, and marry, younger women. Females who have a youthful appearance, which would include a good skin, firm breasts and long thick hair,[20] also do well in the attractiveness stakes – you knew this anyway. All this to satisfy the evolutionary driver: 'To breed is to succeed.'

We have to remember here that physical attractiveness is also very much affected by culture and era. Even without her arms Venus de Milo was the beauty of her time (in 120 BC) and yet has a very small bust; while England's hero John Bull is very portly when compared to the svelte male models of today, yet both were considered attractive in their day.

Faces

Now, surprise, surprise, of course men are attracted to women who can bear them lots of healthy babies and women are attracted to men who appear strong enough to protect all those babies, yet both men and women are more impressed with the face[21] of a potential mate rather than any other part of the body.

We naturally have a preference for certain types of faces over others, with usually such faces being those of our family members. This may explain why you may be attracted to others who resemble them – a phenomena known as assortative mating.

For the female, having a youthful face is the most significant fertility sign to a male. This certainly explains why a woman will spend a fortune on make-up and another fortune in time applying it to look much younger than they are. This idea is captured in the cruel quote by the slightly misogynous Oscar Wilde:

'A man's face is his autobiography. A woman's face is her work of fiction.'

This may have been true in Wilde's time, but now grooming products for men come rushing out of the closet again, long after the beauty spot antics which were made fashionable by Prince George's favourite, Beau Brummell, at the end of the eighteenth century. Fast forward to 1980 and we find more and more items are available to enhance the male visage. Today there are 40 million entries in Google for 'men's make-up'.

Concerning attractiveness, psychologists at the University of New Mexico have actually found that when a woman ovulates she shows a preference for men whose body odour suggested symmetry![22] Makers of men's aftershave and fragrance take note!

Interestingly, a female when ovulating prefers in a male a strong jawline, heavy brows and broad cheekbones, all of which are associated with a high level of testosterone.[23] Men, if you do not have this type of face, all is not lost, because in early follicular or luteal phases the chin preference gives way to a good skin, indicating good health over the Marlboro-man look.

Babies of both sexes prefer to look at symmetrical faces[24] than those, shall we say in a kindly way, that are more interesting.

However, physical attractiveness is only one factor out of many that makes us attractive enough to achieve an ongoing relationship and to maintain it. Divorce rates among the beautiful people who inhabit both screen and stage is significantly higher than average. Yes, looks are seductive, but in the long term it is what lies beneath that is the foundation of long relations.

Eyes

Lashed eyes are another sign of health. Besides being the window to the soul, large eyes in women are a definite plus in the looks department and have been for a long time, as Mark Antony found out when he visited Egypt in 41 BC. But here again we can take heart if we are not in the beauty queue when we were made. Cleopatra VII Philopator, although she knew the advantage of eye make-up, was better known in her time for her wit, intelligence and the sweetness of her voice.

Perhaps here while we are talking about the eyes of a female, we should also mention the advice of Victor Hugo when he wrote:

'When a woman is talking to you, listen to what she says with her eyes.'

Although the variation in the maximum size of our pupils is individual, you can check if that special person you have just met finds you attractive by checking the change in their pupil size – providing, of course, you are not both in a dimly lit bar where you both have to dilate your pupils just to be able to see. Because of colour convergence, those with blue eyes are easier to 'read' than brown eyes and for that reason they disclose more of their feelings towards you. In the WASP world where females have more of a choice concerning eye colour, blue eyes are thought to be marginally more attractive than brown.

Our eyes also become somewhat watery when we find someone attractive, which is yet another physiological reaction that is difficult to develop but easy to recognise.

Glasses

Early research found that wearing glasses[25] has an interesting effect on the way that you are perceived. Men are rated more intelligent and also serious, conventional and hardworking, but less manly. Women are rated more intelligent, honest, serious and sometimes 'dizzy'.

Which version of the same lady do you find more attractive?

In their alter egos as Superman, Spiderman, Superwoman and Wonder Woman, none of the superheros wear glasses, despite tonnes of testosterone for the first two and an oestrogen explosion for the latter.

For the same reason, we have grey hair and wrinkles after the age of 40, we begin to notice that our ability to focus on near objects begins to decline, and by that age, as our arms are fixed in length, glasses are the only way to go. This is the onset of presbyopia – such an unkind word, from first the Greek and then the Latin, meaning 'old man eyes'. No wonder 'men and women do not make passes at people with glasses'. I tell people that my glasses are to make them more attractive.

brilliant tip

Take off your glasses to appear more attractive and younger because for most of us our vision declines with increasing age.[26]

Breasts

Certainly in Western culture, large breasts are attractive to men because the research suggests a top breast to under breast ratio indicates that a female enjoys a greater level of estradiol, a sex hormone critical for fertility. Breast position is also an excellent and obvious sign of fertility[27] and men, as we all know, at a basic level are driven to reproduce, which explains all those vain attempts at surreptitious staring.

Male and female voices

Here we go back to Darwin[28] again when he wrote:

'Although the sounds emitted by animals of all kinds serve many purposes, a strong case can be made out that vocal organs were primarily used and perfected in relation to the propagation of the species.'

Most men show an enhanced preference for women with high-pitched voices – remember Ms Monroe when she sang

'Happy Birthday, Mr President ...'? Women, on the other hand – although not so strongly affected by voice pitch – by and large prefer men with deep voices.

Interestingly, women with a higher pitched voice are also blessed with a more attractive face and in men it is the reverse. All this is to do with hormone levels – mainly testosterone – because it suggests dominance (or lack of), fertility, health and attractiveness.

Skin

Skin is the body's window on health, and healthy people are attractive people. Even in some primates their skin indicates social-sexual availability to potential mates. Because skin blood perfusion reflects cardiovascular health,[29] the fitter we are the more attractive we are, and this holds true for both sexes. At a very basic level both males and females want/need to procreate and a fit person is the best bet to satisfy this need.

Have you ever wondered why the higher-ranking women (power, status, resources, etc.) in societies from the US to India and most places in between have, in the main, fairer skins?[30] By and large powerful men prefer fair skin in a female, whilst females of any status are indifferent or have a slight preference for males with a darker skin. This is the basic hair colour protocol for maidens and heroes of the corset-ripper genre of ever-popular romantic novels. The natural outcome of generations of men acting on this sexual proclivity has been fairer and fairer children.

All this might eventually change, with Hollywood enjoying a Mediterranean climate and producing sun-tanned beauties for the screen, and the advent of profitable spray tan parlours and the associated advertising which tell us that 'Bronze is Beautiful'.

Personal aroma

Body odour (BO), even if it is sweet smelling, is a somewhat taboo topic, but it has a very significant place in body language and attractiveness. In all cultures BO resulting from a lack of personal hygiene has a strong adverse effect on another person of either sex, usually resulting in rejection.

What has this to do with attractiveness? Pheromones play a large part in physical attraction, especially the pheromone called androstenone.

Personal scents can attract; fresh sweat on males is attractive to females, not only because of the male pheromone androstenone* but also because it is an indication of good health and virility. However, our personal odour, given off by our pheromones, is as unique as our signatures on our bankcards – much to the chagrin of the escaping prisoner when the dogs pick up and identify his individual scent from all the others on his escape route. We may not be as astute as man's best friend, but 95 per cent of us given personal odour alone can tell whether it originates from a male or a female.

A recent study[31] suggests that women who are exposed to different male sweat scents responded to them differently. Perspiration from men watching 'educational' videos stimulated different parts of the female brain than the sweat produced when men were watching another type of video. This suggests that women can identify, through odour, a man who is interested in her.

---

* Men, please note: androstenol is produced by fresh male sweat and is arousing for women but only for 20 minutes, then exposure to oxygen converts it to androstenone – the locker-room smell – and it will certainly not have the effect you had hoped!

Unfortunately for the males amongst us, women are not as skilled in this area as lepidoptera (moths and butterflies) where some species can, at six miles in any direction, recognise a suitable mate.

For attractiveness, any perfume with musk would appear to be the winner. Women are more sensitive to it than males but even they can detect it in one part per 100,000, and the fairer sex are more likely to respond to it during ovulation since the oestrogen hormone makes the odour very attractive. So if you want to be more physically attractive, go for musk. (See when you should break this rule, on page 50.)

Pheromones

Pheromones* work for bats, pigs, elephants and mice, sending real non-verbal messages to one another indicating fear, membership of a social group, that they are sexy or that they can induce a female to be ready for sex. All this sounds great but, unfortunately, irrespective of your gender preference if you are human you lack the essential equipment to practise this advantage on someone you find attractive. The animals mentioned above, and almost any animal that has fur or hair, have the advantage of a piece of equipment located in their nose which has been christened by scientists as the vomeronasal organ (VNO). Pheromones wafting past this funny sounding organ are recognised and delivered to the brain. Humans also have a VNO but unfortunately, or fortunately, depending on your proclivities at the time, it does not work as well as it should. Rather like our toes – they are there but are not as useful as those of our primate ancestors.

But hope is on the horizon; there has been some research by two Nobel-Prize-winning scientists collaborating at Harvard[32]

---

* Pheromone from the Greek *pherein*, meaning to transfer, and *hormon*, to excite.

that all is not lost – we share a gene with the humble mouse that is essential to pheromone detection – so watch, not smell, this space and don't be taken in just yet by the marketing hype, even if you are looking for a partner.

Legs

Secretly, many women want to make their legs look longer, as longer legs equal greater sex appeal.[33] Many things happen when a girl advances into puberty, but for the male of the species she becomes a potential mate. At the same time the growth hormones kick in, especially in elongation of a females' legs. In the simple male mind, and of course at a sexual level (most males do tend to be very simple beings) long legs equal reproductive readiness.

An example of lordosis in action, but note the arms akimbo, not in aggression, but to lift the bust.

So for women, high heels and, if she can get away with it, a short skirt says to the deep level* of the male brain 'reproductive ready'. Heels give the impression of lordosis, because they give an inward curvature to the spine which in turn pushes the bottom out, which is another sign of post pubescence. As experienced beach Romeos have come to recognise, high heels are not always necessary for lordosis to occur. Most women, if they find a man physically attractive, will curve their back by going up on their toes without being conscious of what they are doing.

Male body language and partnering

Males compete for the attention of the female, so when they are in a pack they will compete for air time. It does not matter what they say, as long as they are reducing the air and vision time of other male suitors. So, like the peacock's sexual display, men want to appear physically bigger;[34] the shoulders go back, the chest is pushed out and the hands are either pronated (with the knuckles turned outward to enhance the 'V' shape) or are placed on the hips.

An evolutionary equation for men

Looking big = Looking strong = Powerful protector = Gain mate = Procreate = Gene survival

As part of his display the male will attempt to stand in front of the female with his feet slightly apart, to increase his physical space as well as cutting off any hope of advance from other males. If she finds him attractive the female will turn towards him, indicating acceptance; if not, he receives the 'cold shoulder' treatment and turns to another possible suitor.

---

* The 'old' brain which sits on top of the spinal column in the base of the skull is sometime referred to as the 'reptilian brain', because all vertebrates from reptiles to mammals have one.

What is the male doing here and how is the female responding?
Answers on pages 224–5.

Of course, the male wants to looks good so he engages in preening behaviour by brushing back his hair, straitening his tie or smoothing some other piece of clothing. (Women in the same circumstances self-preen too.)

Whilst all this is going on his eyes are working overtime – although he has done this many times before – and as he makes his approach the male attempts to hold her gaze. Once in front of the female his eyes will alternate between her eyes and her mouth.

Pupil dilation is not only a sign of a good hand at poker, but also a significant body language sign of physiological attraction. Boy meets girl or girl meets boy, the magic happens and both parties want to see as much of each other as they can, so their pupils dilate. However, pupil dilation is only one sign that indicates you may be attractive to the other person (if you frighten them their eyes will also dilate!), so check for a supporting cluster. If their eyebrows are raised, their shoulder moves out of parallax with yours, and their feet are pointing away from you, you are definitely not as attrative as you thought you were!

Blink rate also increases in the other person when they find you attractive. There are some ladies who enjoy the attraction and attention of men for its own sake and so have become skilled in the flirtatious flutter of the eyelids.

When he feels confident the male will then move from social space to intimate space. He might make an excuse to legitimise this by removing a real or an imagined hair or piece of fluff from the female's shoulder. Or he might lower his voice to encourage the female to lean or come closer so she can hear. If more than a social closeness is maintained he might become bolder and may touch the female on the arm or shoulder in his conversation to illustrate a point or emphasis. If the female does not move back or frown he will then extend his hand to those socially acceptable places.

Female body language and partnering

Females have a much greater armoury of body language when it comes to making themselves attractive. Some say that males are so slow on the uptake they need two or three signals to catch up with the female intuition.

So what does she do? There is a lot of self-touching – not only preening but touching her body, particularly her neck. She also makes herself appear more vulnerable by exposing her neck by stretching it. Whilst doing this she might laugh and throw her head back, which not only exposes her neck but highlights her bust, too.

Unlike the man, who attempts to show off his strength and dominance, the woman engages in the reverse with a limp wrist and her palms facing outwards.

When aroused, female lips engorge with blood, making them more red and fuller. She might emphasise this by licking her lips, which draws attention to this part of the face and their lustre.

As an orifice the mouth is also considered alluring, so she may make an excuse to lick her fingers and/or she may also swallow noticeably when there is nothing in her mouth.

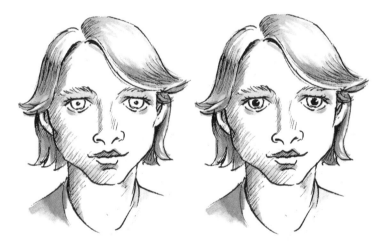

In which of these two pictures of the same woman does she look most attractive? More people will say the picture on the right.

Like the male, the female's eyes too are working overtime, except in a different way. Having managed to secure the social gaze of the male for just a little longer than usual, suggesting an intimate look, she will look down and possibly to the side, finally returning her gaze. She will repeat this submissive sign if the male does not pick up on it the first time around.

Again, just like the male, if she finds a male that she sees who is attractive or pleasing, her pupils will enlarge and the male will respond likewise to this signal without even knowing it. Not so long ago ladies who enjoyed just the attention of men for its own sake, or wished to show to her friends how popular she was, might put a very little juice of the poisonous belladonna berry into her eyes which would make her pupils dilate. In Italian *belladonna* means 'beautiful woman'.

Humour

Strange as it may seem, we all know but may not understand why humour is so sexy. Just look at the personal ads in next Sunday's paper to notice how so many people want GSH (good sense of humour) in a partner. Humour outranks physical attractiveness in finding a life partner.[35]

The company you keep

Most parents become concerned when their children mix with bad or inappropriate company, especially during the teenage years when peer group cultural cloning has such an influence on social behaviour and values of the young. It is natural to judge people by the company they keep. Long ago the Book of Proverbs suggested: 'He that walketh with wise men shall be wise' (13:20), and later: 'A man that hath friends must show himself friendly' (18:24).

This phenomenon also explains people's aspirations to be part of the 'in crowd'; to be seen with the 'beautiful people' or walk in the 'corridors of power'. It also works in commerce to make an organisation more attractive. Most firms, and certainly consultancies, will list their clients as a way of demonstrating their bona fides.

brilliant tip

So to increase your attractiveness quotient, align yourself with attractive people.[36]

And when it all comes together over time

Touching socially acceptable parts of the body would be a good indication of the desire for intimacy. By the time it has got this far men are driven by their feelings and desires. For women, whilst light petting might be physically enjoyable, common sense kicks in whilst she reviews future consequences and options before she gives permission to continue. Females, as every male knows, will reject advanced physical intimacy if they do not feel comfortable or they still have reservations about the person. This includes possible future scenarios if petting continues.*

If these are no issues for the female then intimacy is allowed to become mutual. Mock physical play and fighting makes touch socially acceptable and so the relationship matures. Deliberate physical contact, usually kissing, is the opening act for reciprocal intimacy. Increased mutual personal touching occurs in the sequence from peripheral to central, and consummation is enjoyed. It is a dance where both must move together in time and action; too fast or too slow can have disappointing outcomes for one or both of the romantic pair.

---

* With the advent of the sexual revolution of the 1960s there has been an increasing relaxation of these reservations, as sex is a basic drive for both men and women.

Summary

Many of the following features of attractiveness are inherited and difficult to fake, but please remember that there are very few individuals – male or female – who possess, thankfully for 99.999 per cent of us, all these genetically inherited qualities.

Remember also, here we discount the huge effect of personality and are only concerned with the physical aspects of both male and female.

For females

Preferably slim, with thick, healthy hair and clear skin, she will have neonate features, with a small chin, small nose and big eyes, and a post-pubescent body. Moving to the face, she will have high eyebrows, large high cheek bones over narrow cheeks, under which there is the potential for a huge smile, and a higher-pitched voice; then lower still a significant bust and a slim but hourglass figure supported by longer-than-average legs. This would make the perfect physical female from a traditional

Both these women show features of attractiveness. On the left large eyes and small chin, on the right an almost perfectly symmetrical face.

male viewpoint. Fortunately, according to the Body Shop, there are only six women in the world that have achieved all the above and, at the time of writing, this is out of a total world population of 3,428,196,000 females. For those who like figures (no pun intended) females have a 1 in 571,366,000 chance of being viewed as physically perfect. Why else would Photoshop be so popular with fashion photographers?

For males

For those who have not had the benefit of any input from Hollywood for the past 20 years, the perfect male is taller than average, with a 'V'-shaped hairless torso, supported by a trim and firm bottom. Moving upwards there should be a smiling, symmetrical, clean-shaven face revealing a strong chin and a deep voice. A good head of hair helps if you are under 40, but beyond that it diminishes in importance.

 recap*

Females:

- Smile as much as you can.
- If you must wear perfume, have a musk base, if it suits you.
- If you have thick hair, grow it; if you have thin hair, cut it.
- Blonde hair will make you look younger.
- Do not wear glasses.
- Look after your skin as much as possible.
- Be an expert in make-up.

▶

* Please take into account that this summary for this chapter is concerned with body language and attraction, because read out of context I am sure it could offend both men and women!

Males:

- Stay around females as much as possible (propinquity).
- Use stacks of deodorant when and where necessary.
- Smile as much as you can.
- Stand tall.
- Exercise to look fit.
- Develop your shoulders and chest.
- Develop and use humour.

Just one more thing before we move on to the signs of attraction. Did you know that besides shows of affection:

'Males kiss in the hope of having sex or to say sorry, females kiss to check how the relationship is going'?

The signs of attraction

21 early signs that the other person (either male or female) finds you attractive

1 Does the person frequently attempt to catch your eye?

2 Does the person attempt to stand in front of you?

3 Does the person smile a lot?

4 Does the person attempt to amuse?

5 Does the person have their feet pointing towards you?

6 Does the person groom and touch themselves frequently?

7 Does the person attempt to find a reason to touch you?

8 Does the person laugh easily and often when they are with you?

9 Does the person hold their arms to their sides?

10 Does the person frequent the same places as you?

11 Does the person pay more attention to you than others when in the company of others?

12 Does the person lick their lips more frequently than others?

13 Does the person move into your personal space?

14 Does the person have an initial high blink rate?

15 Does the person breathe more quickly in your presence?

16 Does the person mirror you?

17 Does the person have significant eye dilation, especially when surroundings are bright?

18 Does the person speak more softly to increase intimacy/ draw you closer?

19 Does the person discuss opportunities to see you again before you part?

20 Does the person give you their best smile when you separate?

21 Does the person's handshake seem slightly prolonged?

21 early signs that she finds you attractive

1 Does she let you stand in front of her?

2 Does she look at you, and when you catch her eye for the first time does she look down?

3 Does she arch her back when she first sees you?

4 Does she go on to her tip toes when she first sees you?

5 Does she expose her neck when she laughs at something you said?

6 Does she put her hand on her neck and/or under her hair?

7 Does she rub her foot behind the calf of her other leg?

8 Does she stand occasionally with her legs slightly apart?

9 Does she toss her head so that her hair flicks away?

10 Does she touch you whilst with her friends?

11 Does she, when sitting, turn slightly side on, enabling you to see all of her?

12 Does she, when sitting, cross one leg over the leg that is closest to you?

13 Does she, when you are not sitting next to her, have her knees pointing towards you?

14 Does she allow one shoe to dangle off her foot when sitting when her legs are crossed?

15 Does she adjust her clothing, especially round her waist, to show off her figure?

16 Does she not show annoyance if she catches you taking a sneaky look at her bust?

17 Does she turn and expose her neck?

18 Does she laugh or giggle a lot when you try to be funny?

19 Does she roll her hips when she walks towards you?

20 Does she lean forward when you lean forward?

21 Does she look at you when you walk away from her? (Ask a friend to observe!)

In Victorian times it was much easier; single maidens as they passed a male who, shall we say, was slow on the uptake, just happened to accidentally drop their handkerchief and the male felt compelled to be a gentleman and return it to the maiden, who would then fain surprise at her gaucherie. At the annual Hunt Ball (the posh equivalent of a singles' event but arranged by pickie parents), if a lady – they did not allow women in – caught your eye and then hid behind her fan the gallant gentleman – they did not allow men in either – could count on being the last swain on the dance card.

21 early signs that he finds you attractive

1   Does he make himself taller?

2   Does he puff out his chest?

3   Does he attempt to increase his 'physical' zone?

4   Does he put his hands on his hips?

5   Does he keep looking at you?

6   Does he nod his head up and down slightly when you are talking?

7   Does he keep his arms away from his chest?

8   Does he attempt to interrupt other males when they are talking to you?

9   Does he make eye contact all the time you are speaking?

10 Does he give an encouraging smile or laugh at what you say?

11 Does he attempt physically to block other males from moving close to you?

12 Does he attempt to move into your private space?

13 Does he find an excuse to touch your hand, elbow, arm or shoulder?

14 Does he move his head slightly to his right when you are talking?

15 Does he try to prolong conversations with you?

16 Does he sneak an occasional look at your bust?

17 Does he track you as you move through the room? (Ask a friend to observe!)

18 Does he offer to do things for you? (Getting a drink or chair for you, opening a door, etc.)

19 Does he try to sit close to you or next to you rather than opposite you?

20 Does his tic (verbal or physical) become more noticeable?

21 Does he attempt to walk with you when you leave?

In medieval times it was easier because all the champion of the joust had to do was to present to the lady of his heart's desire his colours and, with the king's approval, the deal was sealed.

So what does all this mean … ?

To get all this into proportion, as important as attractiveness is, most of what we have been dealing with here has pertinence only to first impressions, and fortunately ongoing relations and those that grow into intimate relations take far more into consideration.

When we first meet someone we reveal very little of ourselves. Much of our behaviour is governed by social/cultural norms, with personal individuality kept at a minimum. We smile a lot, agree a lot, and nod our heads a lot, wanting to appear an agreeable person.

(As an aside, the desire to make a good first impression is also one of the many reasons that makes interviewing such an unreliable technique for employee selection. The parties on both sides of the office desk are on their best behaviour; candidates presenting themselves in the best way they can and recruiters presenting their organisation in the best way they can, which explains the frequent disappointment of both parties three months later.)

As relationships move on we begin to reveal more of our psychological apparel. According to Maslow's hierarchy of needs,[37] once we have and have satisfied our need for air, water, food and safety, then sex and social needs come to the fore. It is here that most of the body language of attraction comes into play. To survive, ongoing and permanent relationships demand far more of the couple than just the satisfaction of the sex drive or to be socially acceptable to our peers. Higher aspects of ourselves, such as interpersonal behaviour, our personality, our values and spirituality – all those significant aspects that make us truly human – are necessary not only in permanent relationships but in both life and work.

One of the essential criteria for success is the strength of your interpersonal skills. Socially you need to have empathy, understanding, generosity, respect and, at work, social acceptance, influence and persuasiveness, since it is hard for you to get to the top without being able to get others to do things for you and for them to be happy and contented to do so. It is difficult to manifest these competences and traits without a portfolio of non-verbal skills and an understanding of body language.

Now we might not be as attractive as we wish but in life it is very important to be able to influence others, so this is our next topic.

'I can win an argument on any topic, against any opponent. People know this, and steer clear of me at social events. Often, as a sign of their great respect, they don't even invite me.'

Dave Barry, comedian

References

1 Kinsey, A. (1948), *Sexual Behaviour in the Human Male*.
2 Dion, K., Berscheid, E. and Walster, E. (1972), 'What is beautiful is good', *Journal of Personality and Social Psychology* 24 (3).
3 Glaap, A. R. (1999), *A Guided Tour Through Ayckbourn Country*.

4 Cash, T. F., Gillen, B. and Burns, D. S. (1977), 'Sexism and "beautyism" in personnel consultant decision making', *Journal of Applied Psychology* 62.

5 *Ibid.*

6 Etcoff, N. (2000), *Survival of the Prettiest: The Science of Beauty.*

7 Barber, N. (1995), 'The evolutionary psychology of physical attractiveness: Sexual selection and human morphology', *Ethology and Sociobiology* 16.

8 Hatfield, E. and Sprecher, S. (1986), *Mirror, Mirror ... The Importance of Looks in Everyday Life.*

9 Liche, M. D. and Zell, E. (2009), 'Social attractiveness and blame', *Journal of Applied Social Psychology* 39 (9).

10 DeSantis, A. and Kayson, W. A. (1997), 'Defendants' characteristics of attractiveness, race, and sex and sentencing decisions', *Psychological Reports* 81(2).

11 Brossard, J. (1932), 'Residential propinquity as a factor in mate selection', *American Journal of Sociology.*

12 Allen, T. J. and Henn, G. (2006), *The Organization and Architecture of Innovation Technology.*

13 Dixon, B. J. et al. (2009), 'Studies of human physique and sexual attractiveness', *Archives of Sexual Behavior* 19.

14 Discovery Channel UK, January 2007.

15 Sherrow, V. (2006), *Encyclopaedia of Hair: A cultural history.*

16 Sailer, S. (2005), *Blondes Have Deeper Roots.*

17 Cash, T. F. (1990), 'Losing hair, losing points', *Journal of Applied Social Psychology* 20.

18 Smith, T. W. (2006), 'American sexual behavior: Trends, sociodemographic differences, and risk behavior', *GSS Topical Report* 25.

19 Stunkard, A. J. and Wadden, T. A. (1985), 'Social and psychological consequences of obesity', *Annals of Internal Medicine* 103.

20 Sherrow, V., *Ibid.*

21 Zaidel, D. W., Aarde, S. M. and Baig, K. (2005), 'Appearance of symmetry, beauty, and health in human faces', *Brain and Cognition* 57.

22 Palermo, P. (2008), *Symmetry? Could This be the Answer to the Age Old Question; 'What is Beauty?'*

23 Buss, D. (2003), *The Evolution of Desire*; and 'Sexual dimorphism and health', Proceedings of the Royal Society (Biological Sciences).

[24] Slater, A. and Lewis, M. (eds) (2007), *Introduction to Infant Development* 2nd edition.

[25] Thornton, G. R. (1944), 'The effect of wearing glasses on personality traits of persons seen briefly', *Journal of Applied Psychology* 28.

[26] Hamid, P. N. (1972), 'Some effects on dress clues on observational accuracy', *Journal of Social Psychology* 86 (2).

[27] Buss, D. (2005), *The Handbook of Evolutionary Psychology*.

[28] Darwin, C. (1871), *The Descent of Man and Selection in Relation to Sex*.

[29] Stephen, I. (2008), 'Skin colour signals human health', a paper presented at St Andrews University.

[30] Frost, P. (2005), *Fair Women, Dark Men: The Forgotten Roots of Racial Prejudice*.

[31] Denise Chen of Rice University, Texas, reported in *The Daily Telegraph*, 29 December 2009.

[32] In 2004 Richard Axel of the Howard Hughes Medical Institute, New York, and Linda Buck of the Fred Hutchinson Cancer Research Centre, Seattle, jointly received the Nobel Prize for Medicine.

[33] Pierce, C. A. (1996), 'Body height and romantic attraction', *Social Behavior and Personality* 24.

[34] Rikowski, A. (1981), 'Physical attractiveness: The influence of selected torso parametres', *Archives of Sexual Behavior* 10 (1).

[35] Sprecher, S. and Regan, P. S. (2002), 'Partner preferences in romantic relationships and friendships', *Journal of Social and Personal Relationships* 19.

[36] Kernis, D. A. and Wheeler, K. E. (1981), 'Beautiful friends and ugly stangers', *Journal of Personality and Social Psychology Bulletin* 7.

[37] Maslow, A. H. (1954), *Motivation and Personality*.

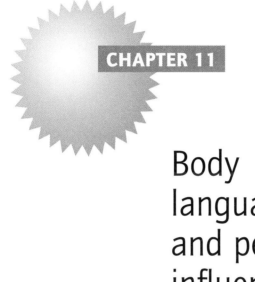

CHAPTER 11

Body language and personal influence

Gaining what you need

Everything we need on this earth, except perhaps the air we breathe, has a limited supply. We can use personal influence to achieve from these limited resources what we need and, if we are fortunate, what we want. Our physical needs, our emotional and our social needs are significantly affected by how skilled we are in being able to influence and persuade others, from close family to total strangers.

brilliant definition

Influence (noun)

The ability to persuade another to accept willingly a predetermined outcome, action, view point or attitude from that which they originally held, by potency of argument rather than employing overt or covert pressure.

When we attempt to influence a person or a group, we make a deliberate attempt to change, to shape, to reinforce or alter the views of others.[1] To influence someone or to get them to change their mind is not an easy task. Many people's minds and views are like concrete: all mixed up and then set hard.

'There are some people, who if they don't already know, you can't tell them.'

Yogi Berra, American baseball player

It is also important to remember that people very much 'own' their views. If they are challenged it involves not only logic but also has an effect on their egos, so to challenge them directly is also to challenge them as a person.

Changing someone's mind usually takes the following slow process because people say 'No', before they say 'Maybe', before they say 'Yes'.

Much of what we have said in terms of creating a great first impression and being effectively assertive is applicable here. There are some additional points which need to be made, particularly when addressing groups. These are most relevant when the group to whom you are presenting to could be somewhat adversarial before you even open your mouth.

There has been a great deal of work examining the variables that facilitate influence and persuasion. Not surprisingly, one of the most powerful variables is high expertise[2] – the more you are thought to be an expert, the more likely you are to persuade another to your argument.

It was a long time ago, in 1960 in fact, when the significance of body language made an incredible impact on psychology. In that year there was a US presidential showdown between two candidates which was broadcast both on television and radio. It was significant because those who listened to the debate on the radio thought that Richard Nixon gave the best performance of the two but, surprisingly, those who watched the debate on television voted in favour of Jack Kennedy.

Nixon, with his now-famous five o'clock shadow, dull grey suit and a preponderance to perspire, did not look as presidential as Kennedy, who sat with his legs crossed and hands at rest whereas Nixon's body revealed signs of tenseness, exaggerated by gripping his chair and a blink rate that could only be matched by a humming bird – not the most confident of looks.

> 'I believe that I spent too much time in the last campaign on substance and too little on appearance.'
>
> Nixon, after he had lost.

That debate brought home to all professional speakers, politicians, barristers, advocates, lobbyists, motivational speakers and some university lecturers (and perhaps a few clergy) that it is not just the words you utter that are important but the support of congruent body language plus the 'style' in which the words are delivered. Words are diamonds which need appropriate body language as a setting to show off their brilliance.

When we have to make a speech or a presentation most of us will spend the bulk of our time making sure that our facts are correct, so we focus on the substance of what we wish to say, hoping that the strength of our propositions and the elegance of our arguments will win the day.

We know that the Nixon style is insufficient because to influence someone requires not only the cognitive brain work of logic and rationality, but also the emotional side of smiles and confident body and hand movements – that is to say corresponding body language. To persuade and influence, it is imperative that speech and body support each other.[3] Think of it as nitrogen and glycerin, which are reasonably safe when spearated but when mixed together become a very powerful expolosive we know as nitroglycerine. As we have discovered from the Mehrabian research (see page 6), we tend to accept more readily the veracity of NVC than what is actually being said, but for a 'nitroglycerine effect' there must be both if we wish to change people's minds.

The good news is that, unlike our personality traits, which tend to be fixed from around the age of four, we can learn to both control and use our NVC appropriately and so improve the power of our impression management.

We now turn to cover some of the skills of influencing.

Dress

We trust people who are like ourselves. An important way of showing that we are like those whom we wish to influence is through our dress and style.

 **example**

In the consultancy we have a very brilliant intern but we cannot use her when we counsel and coach senior executives, although she is very competent to do so, because there are two major difficulties. First, she is so much younger than the executive, but secondly, and perhaps more importantly, she is very creative in her sartorial fashion tastes (we do not enforce a dress code on the consultancy for back-of-house employees) with the obvious result that an executive is turned off before she even opens her young mouth (see first impressions on pages 33–51). This style problem would be just the same if the intern was a fresh male psychology post graduate.

Make eye contact

Eye contact promotes conviction, seriousness and the impor-tance of what you have to say. From the body language of those who are listening to you, it will help you check their understanding, their interest, engagement and their potential willingness to be persuaded.

If you want to persuade someone you must look them in the eye. It does not matter if you want to convince a jury of your innocence, or hitch a ride, or solicit charity donations on the street or convince your partner that their tummy/bottom does not look big in last year's trousers; you must look them in the eye.

Research confirms that witnesses are thought to be less credible when they avert their eyes when the barrister questions them.[4]

So here are some more suggestions that you can add to your skill portfolio which will make you appear even more of an expert.

Get their attention

You cannot influence anyone who is not paying you attention.

When speaking to groups of people, stand tall and straight, face your audience, balance yourself, look at everyone and stay quiet until they and you are ready to begin. If you are waiting for people to arrive, stay seated until everyone has arrived then get up and move to the centre of the room and follow the above process.

brilliant example

There was once a famous horse whisperer who was renowned for his reputation for using kindness when starting (breaking) and training horses. Because of the fame of the horse whisperer an owner with a very expensive horse took his mount to him to receive advanced dressage training.

When the horse was taken into the ménage, the owner was horrified when the famous trainer whacked the horse hard on the rump. 'I thought you were gentle in your training methods!' said the aghast owner. 'I am', said the whisperer, 'But now I have his full attention!'

You cannot influence anyone who is not paying you attention, but I would not recommend the horse whisperer approach or that of the clergyman who made his way up into the pulpit only to begin his sermon with an expletive. No one went to sleep just in case he did it again, and his sermon was the talk of the village.

brilliant tip

When wanting to start your presentation, stand, move into your presentation space, look at the participants and wait. Just keep waiting and eventually a silence will descend on the room. Most people in groups find silence difficult, but now you have their attention. This is the time to begin. Your presence and silence, plus your look, will act like a conductor's baton when bringing the orchestra to attention.

Take the high ground

Height, as we have mentioned, has many advantages, but being above the person you wish to influence will give you a distinct advantage. When presenting, even to groups as small as four people, it is useful to stand. Being higher gives you two advantages: it makes you look more confident in what you are saying; you also appear to have more authority and, believe it or not, 66 per cent[5] of us prefer to be compliant, especially if the person appears to have authority.[6]

Be fluent

People are fluent when they know what they are talking about or presenting. So although you can slightly vary the pitch of your voice (if you go too high it is taken as a sign of nervousness), to avoid a boring monotone you should maintain your fluency.

Speak slowly

Whilst speaking quickly gives the impression of enthusiasm, it is important to remember that when you want to influence someone it is paramount that they understand and are able to consider the position that you want them to take. Whilst the mind can always work faster than anyone's rate of speech, you do not want their mind to go walkabout, considering one point only to miss the next three points of your proposition.

For your message to succeed you must be enthusiastic not frenetic; you cannot persuade unless you are persuaded, but do not be in a rush, just speak slightly quicker than your normal rate. Many an excellent candidate has not been selected for a position because they have not given the interviewer enough time to reflect on the content of what is being said and to mentally match it to the competency requirements demanded by the position.

Additionally, speaking too quickly will cause you to take quick shallow breaths. Your body may interpret this as anxiety and, guess what, that anxiety increases the speed of speech; and so it goes on, if it is not checked, to hyperventilation and a real anxiety attack.

People with authority speak slowly because they are used to being listened to and being obeyed. By anticipating and expecting compliance they achieve it.

We have already mentioned how compliant most of us are and it was frighteningly demonstrated in the famous Milgram experiments* of 1974 at Yale. In 2010, when this experimental design

---

* The essence of the Milgram experiments and this reality game was to apply shocks to a person (who actually, unbeknown to the player, was an actor) if they gave the wrong answers. If the player appeared to be concerned about the 'pain' that they were inflicting, they were told in a very slow and measured way such statements as 'You are required to continue'; 'Just continue'. This they did, increasing the voltage till the confederate subject feigned actual death when they applied 460 volts.

was repeated on a reality show *Le jeu de la mort* and aired on the state-owned France 2 channel, the director said, 'We were amazed to find that 81 per cent of the participants obeyed the sadistic orders of the television presenter, which were delivered in a slow and paced way'.

Now there might have been experimental flaws here but the message is clear – when we want to influence, persuade or gain compliance, speak slowly and with all the authority you can muster.

Increase the volume and depth of your voice

Confidence and credibility are conferred on those who can engineer an increased volume in their speaking. There is a real difference between speaking loudly and raising your voice or shouting. A strong voice not only makes you sound more authoritative but, surprisingly, more emotionally stable as well.[7]

A deep voice also helps – just listen to all those voice-overs encouraging us to go and see a particular film; you never see the person speaking but he must look like a bullfrog. It is very rare that you have a female voice-over in film trailers.

Take pauses

After you have made a major point deliberately, pause and sweep the room with your eyes. This has several advantages: it gives emphasis to what has just been said; it gives you an opportunity to see if your listeners are still tracking and taking an interest in your message; it invites questions; and it gives you an opportunity to construct what you are going to say next.

Control 'ums' and 'errs'

When we are thinking what we should say and how we might say it most of us will fill the thinking time between words with 'ums' and 'errs' which indicate a plethora of handicaps including, but not limited to, a lack in fluency, low confidence, nervousness and, perhaps worse, low intelligence.*

> ### brilliant tip
>
> To appear confident it is better to allow yourself small periods of silence between your words when you are thinking, rather than fill the gaps with 'ums' and 'errs'. We mention the helpful 'ums' and 'errs' or 'minimal encouragers' later (see page 181).

At meetings

As you have probably noticed at meetings, those who have higher status in job title, knowledge, experience, etc., are far more relaxed. Minions who come lower in the pecking order have a tendency to show 'postural restraint'.[8] At worst this would be sitting as if your back was tied to a broomstick, which can be interpreted either as anger or insecurity,[9] whilst our betters appear far more relaxed and show 'postural freedom'.

The advice here is to be relaxed without being slovenly, alert without being intense.

> ### brilliant tip
>
> It is not always what you say; it is the way that you say it!

---

* Fluency is a good indication of intelligence along with the use of words over two syllables and number of imbedded clauses employed in a sentence. This is not to say that individuals who are naturally slow of speech are less intelligent – in the main introverts like to think through what they are going to say – but it is rare for a person who speaks quickly to be intellectually challenged in any way.

brilliant example

At question time in the House of Commons, government ministers, and especially prime ministers, somehow manage to lean on the dispatch box and look confident whilst ordinary MPs, especially the recently elected, stand bolt upright to make their speeches or deliver their questions. Who looks the more nervous; who looks the more confident?

Move your arms not your body

When presenting to groups, stand still. People run when they are fearful; people keep changing their stance when they are anxious. Not only that, but what is interesting here is that the body also affects the mind, so if our physical bodies are agitated we too become mentally agitated, since the mind and the body feed off each other.

In public influencing, rather than one to one (see below), use of the arms and hands can illustrate, emphasise and give colour to what you are saying – rather like the conductor of an orchestra but without the exaggerated upper body movements. Make sure, too, that your arm movements are in sync with what you are saying, otherwise you will confuse your listener, who will pay more attention to your movements than to your words.

Make eye contact (again)

Just as in one-to-one discussions, people in groups want to be addressed as individuals, so continual eye contact with as many people as possible is important. By looking at people you are inviting them to be personally involved with your message and therefore they can be more easily influenced and persuaded.

Hands

We use our hands to make signals such as 'thumbs up', fore-finger and thumb pressed together to indicate 'OK' and we clap to show appreciation, but these are all conscious body movements. Strictly speaking, these signs are not body language. Body language includes such movements as our hands moving when we are anxious so that they are ready to protect ourselves, using your hands to get rid of excess energy, or nervous 'tics' such as running your fingers through your hair. Unlike the thumbs-up sign, we do these gestures without thinking.

Powerful and/or confident people, both in one-to-one or small group situations, do not move their hands in an exaggerated way (public speaking is different). The joke is:

Q 'When does a General move his arms?'

A 'Only when he salutes the Commander in Chief!'

Has anybody ever seen the Queen wave her arms about except when she is in the royal carriage or limousine? Even then it is only a low wave from the royal elbow. Presenting himself for the first time to the waiting crowds, Pope Benedict XVI, who was not known for being demonstrative, lifted both his hands way above his head, somewhat reminiscent of Italian footballers. His fellow cardinals who knew him well, so it is said, gasped in total amazement. Even Pope John Paul II, perhaps one of the most extrovert of recent popes, never thrust his hands straight above his head in the same way and certainly not when he was elected and soon after appeared to the adoring crowds in the Piazza di San Pietro. So social positions are culturally required or perceived to include elements of restraint in order to maintain an air of authority and perhaps an element of mystery.

Steepling

'Steepling' is the most powerful non-verbal sign you can make with your hands. This action involves the tips of your fingers of both hands lightly touching the corresponding digit; do this now and you will see why it is called steepling.

Even the Pope steeples.

When with a friend, stand upright, steeple your hands and bring them apart by about 5cm then revert to steepling again. Do this several times and ask your friend 'Who am I impersonating?'

Answers will range from Prince Charles to Barack Obama, Mikhail Gorbachev or Donald Trump.

You may also remember Lieutenant Colonel Oliver North's superb performance as he made his Congressional statement concerning the Iran-Contra political scandal in the late 1980s.[10] What is the common denominator here? Power. And what is the close partner of power? Confidence. So practise steepling as you make your transitions ever upward through your personal and career aspirations.[11]

Steepling is also appropriate because if both your palms are parallel with the ground it suggests dominance or aggression and, remembering those statues of Buddha or the paintings of Jesus, palms facing upwards suggest not only openness but also submission. When you steeple your palms at 90 degrees you are not being a threat or submissive.

brilliant tip

If you are making a presentation whilst standing and you want to appear authoritative but also relaxed, put both palms pointing forwards on the table, not more than shoulder width apart, and lean towards your audience slightly. Once you have made your point, move back to your original position.

Once you have done this two or three times your audience will expect something significant in what you are about to say when you next repeat the movement.

Questions and interruptions

Sales people, who are professional influencers, welcome questions and challenges because that indicates that what they have been saying has registered but just needs further refinement or explanation. Someone cannot ask you a question unless they have listened to you. Consequently, questions are to be encouraged and there is a non-verbal technique to encourage this.

This might sound silly but it is certainly worth trying. When you invite questions from your listeners, at the first question, unless your audience is huge, sit down and answer it. When you need to continue speaking, just stand up. When you have invited questions two or three times and sat down to answer them you will have trained your audience to know that when you sit down it is their turn to ask questions. Also, your listeners, through your body language and without knowing why, will feel that they have more ownership of the communication process and thus may be more easily persuaded.

Frequently in group situations there is one person, usually for reasons of personal power or because they want to impress you with their knowledge, who will continually interrupt or make inappropriate challenges.

brilliant tip

Do not look at the person who is continually interrupting you as you present. If and when an unwanted interruption comes, rotate your body slightly away from the person, giving them the equivalent of the presenter's 'cold shoulder' as you answer. Your body language is saying 'Be quiet' but you cannot be accused of being rude or aggressive.

Do not show any emotion as that might only encourage the person. Quote to yourself a variation of President Lincoln's famous saying:

'You can please some of the people all of the time,
you can please all of the people some of the time,
but you cannot please all of the people all of the time.'

Personal space

Owning a large physical space indicates power; this not only works for executive offices and executive cars, but also for people. Call it gravitas, call it charisma, but if someone has it people give them space.

There are various ways of enlarging your personal space. Some American CEOs have this down to a fine art. Whilst at meetings they put their arms akimbo (on their hips) or behind their heads, and also stretch their legs out in front of them or rest them on the table. In this way they are saying to their subordinates: 'I am king of the castle'.

brilliant recap

So if you wish to be influential, especially in group situations:

- Dress in the same style as those you wish to persuade, or the style of the most senior person.
- Gain the person(s) attention.
- Where possible, be higher than those you wish to persuade.
- Take up as much physical space as you can to show confidence and authority.
- Be fluent.
- Speak slowly when there is new information and quickly when you want to show enthusiasm.

- Pause frequently to facilitate and check comprehension.
- Increase the volume of your voice and, if you can, put timbre in your voice.
- Maintain eye contact with as many people as possible.
- Keep your body still.
- Make sure that any arm movements are in sync with what you are saying.
- Do not touch your face.
- Learn to steeple, especially when under pressure.
- Encourage questions to facilitate ownership of what you are saying.
- Show positive emotion if someone challenges you.

References

[1] Miller, G. R. (1980), 'On being persuaded: some basic distinctions', in Roloff, M. E. and Miller G. R. (eds), *Persuasion: New directions in theory and research:* 11–27.

[2] Cialdini, R. B. and Goldstein, N. J. (2004), 'Social influence: compliance and conformity', *Annual Review of Psychology* 55.

[3] Costanzo, M. (1992), 'Verban and non-verbal cues and their effects on confidence and performance', *Journal of Educational Psychology* 84.

[4] Hemsy, G. D. et al. (1978), 'The effect of looking behaviour on credibility', *Journal of Applied Social Psychology* 8.

[5] Blass, T. (2004), *The Man who Shocked the World*.

[6] Milgrim, S. (1974), *Obedience to Authority: An Experimental View*.

[7] Aronovich, C. D. (1976), 'The voice of personality', *Journal of Personality and Social Influence* 33.

[8] Burgoon, J. K. et al. (1996), *Non-verbal Communication: The Unspoken Dialogue*.

[9] Knapp, M. L. and Hall, J. A. (2006), *Nonverbal Communication in Human Interaction*.

[10] Bradlee, B. (1998), *Guts and Glory: The Rise and Fall of Oliver North*.

[11] Bixler, S. (1984), *The Professional Image*.

CHAPTER 12

The hidden language of speech

The art of body speech

Whilst not strictly body language, speech structures do come under the category of non-verbal communication.

Appreciating these aspects of speech and how someone structures what they wish to say is an important skill, both in comprehension and in forming your response. We all know the phrase 'It is not what you say it is the way that you say it' and, as Yogi Berra once said:

'You can hear a lot when you listen.'

Speech structure

It would appear that we have preferred ways of structuring the way we deliver information, so for simplicity's sake let's divide them into just three categories.

In the first the speaker – as you can see from the diagram overleaf – begins their presentation by outlining the context and reasons for what they want, which leads slowly towards the point they wish to make or the request they would like approved (the star in the diagram overleaf). In other words, they begin at the beginning, providing reasons and context in the hope that their final point (the star) will be accepted.

This structure is very logical but it is not how some others prefer to deliver information.

Context   Reasons/Justifications   Request/Main point

This process is the most popular. It is also the most powerful because the speaker begins in an area where some, if not all, of the context is known by the listener(s). Your presentation or conversation begins where they are, thus both assisting understanding and hopefully establishing ownership.

If done well, this establishes the current status as a foundation for making your position or request both logical and obvious.

A variation on this could be the insertion of summaries. So the structure would look like:

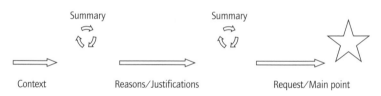

Context   Reasons/Justifications   Request/Main point

Although this is essentially the same structure it provides the listener with a 'head break' and allows the speaker to invite questions before you continue to the next phase.

In the second structure the speaker starts with the main point or request that is in their mind and which they want to get across. Only then will they begin to work backwards, first giving arguments and justifications and concluding with context. So it could be drawn thus:

Main Point/Request   Reasons/Justifications   Context

This second structure, which some people use naturally, can invite difficulties if the point they wish to make is different or, worse, radically different to the status quo. It immediately invites either questions and, if these are not permitted, there are sure to be interruptions.

However, the structure has a huge advantage and is very pragmatic in the case of an emergency. Everyone responds to the word 'FIRE' shouted immediately, so then the person who discovered it can take everyone through the possible location, the various reasons for the outbreak, what four or five consequences could arise if the fire is ignored and, finally, invite questions and a democratic vote to ensure a consensus as to what action would be best to take!

The third speech structure is somewhat more complicated, or creative, in that one initially has difficulty understanding where the other person is coming from, where they are going, or the reasons as to why they are talking to us, apart from, as the Americans say 'shooting the breeze'. But slowly, as you listen and attempt to fathom out where the conversation is going, you begin to be able to separate the 'ambient verbal noise' or flow of consciousness verbiage from the message. The ideas and speech are unwrapped like the parcel in a game of pass the parcel, going round in ever-decreasing circles. Suddenly it all comes together and you understand the conversational kernel or what the other person wants to explain or what they want you to do. If your preferred speech structure is more logical it does take some patience before the 'penny drops'.

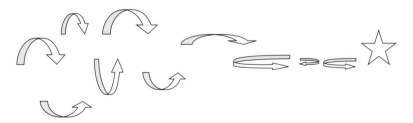

Pleasantaries   Generalities   Growth in specifics   Main point/Request

What is the point of all this? Simply put: if you know how the person prefers to deliver information and if you want to get into rapport, to help them understand what you are saying or you want to persuade them, you can make it easier for them and increase your chance of success if you employ their preferred information delivery system. Easy to say, very difficult to do; sometimes, as you have probably discovered for yourself, it is harder for us to change our own behaviour than it is to change that of others.

Personality and speech

Another way of looking at informational delivery systems is to understand an individual's disposition or type. (It is not appropriate here to outline the full potential of the Myers Briggs Type Indicator®[1] in explaining the effect of disposition on communication structures. Half an hour or so reading some of the excellent summaries on the Internet (just Google MBTI and this will give you a fuller picture).

The MBTI employs categories to help outline different dispositional approaches. Here we only address two of those categories and we begin with how people make decisions, followed by how they like to run or organise their lives.

Decision making: Thinkers (T) and Feelers (F)

Some people are known as 'Thinkers' in the Jungian jargon because of the way in which they make decisions, since they are logical, analytical and firm minded. In other words, they use their heads to make most of their decisions. Some people, known as 'Feelers', prefer to use another strategy when faced with a decision. These people are more comfortable using their heart or their value system to come to a conclusion. By and large their decisions are more humane, empathetic and tender-hearted.

Organising life: Judgers (J) and Perceivers (P)

Judgers tend to be controlled, disciplined and organised in their lives, whereas Perceivers are more spontaneous and free-spirited; preferring to wait and see what the future brings before making a decision is far more appealing than having a firm plan of operation. Judgers like closure and completion so that they can move on, whereas Perceivers like decisions to be made as late as possible because you never know if there might be a new circumstance or opportunity.

Disposition and communication

As you can see, should a person with a TJ (Thinker/Judger) disposition be in conversation with a FP (Feeler/Perceiver) personality they will be like two ships at night in deep fog, with neither vessel having the advantage of radar.

When a TJ asks a direct question, because of their disposition they want a 'Yes' or 'No' answer, but if the person is an FP they are almost incapable of responding just in the affirmative or negative. The FP will find it almost impossible to give a one-word answer. Much to the frustration of the TJ, the FP will give context, circumstances, the place, the time and other peripheral information they can think of before giving a direct answer. Conversely, an FP wife married to a TJ husband will be driven half mad by his monosyllabic responses.

Unfortunately, when someone has a different way of responding there is a tendency to think that they are being awkward, difficult or, at worst, just like a man/woman, and so the relationship either continues as an irritant to both parties or it breaks down completely, to the loss of both people. Ken Blanchard (he of the One-Minute Manager fame) said: 'None of us is as smart as all of us.' Here the person is not being difficult, they are just different. Just as we are either left-handed or right-handed, one is not better than the other. In life all the 'types' of the MBTI are around 50 per cent of the population (whereas left-handers are in a minority of 8 per cent, which accounted for some of the very unfortunate prejudice and discrimination when we were less civilised).

Once you have worked out the dispositional profile of the person you have just met or with whom you are working (and it is not that difficult) you have a great opportunity for developing a mutually profitable relationship.

(There are, of course, variations on the above, with people who enjoy TP and FJ dispositions. Should you find this interesting and useful, use the Internet to find out more about MBTI and also a useful variation, the 'Keirsey Indicator', which is somewhat simpler.)

Speech and physical tics

When Hillary Clinton left her seat in the Senate for greater things, John F. Kennedy's daughter, Caroline, with that wonderful political heritage, made a bid to be elected in Hillary's place. Unfortunately, in an interview with *The New York Times*[2] she lost all hope of winning. It is easy to understand why when you read the following verbatim report of how she responded to being asked if she would be a good Senator:

'So I think in many ways, you know, we want to have all kinds of different voices, you know, representing us, and I think what I bring to it is, you know, my experience as a mother, as a woman, as a lawyer, you know, I've written seven books – two on the Constitution, two on American politics. So obviously, you know, we have different strengths and weaknesses.'

As you could not help but notice, Caroline Kennedy had a severe verbal tic employed, you know, no less than five times in the two sentences above, you know. Probably because, you know, she was nervous about being challenged by a seasoned journalist. You know, under those circumstances it is very easy to lose your fluency, you know.

Physical tics were first recognised as a medical condition and were named after the French neurologist Gilles de la Tourette. These occur when individuals move their bodies suddenly or repeatedly, quickly and uncontrollably and /or make sounds that are involuntary (such as, but not exclusively, gasping, groaning, grunting, gurgling and guttural sounds from the back of the throat). All these are called vocal tics.

Whilst we might not be afflicted by that particular condition, many of us have equivalent verbal tics, sometimes called 'pet words' or 'pet phrases', such as 'you know', 'like', 'in other words', and 'anyway'. We frequently begin sentences with the word 'so' or expand what we have just said with 'what I mean is'.

Should you have a tic it would be to your distinct advantage to curb the habit, since your pet word will probably act as a distraction from your message. Far better for your communication skills to replace the tic with a pause and find alternative ways of saying what you need to say.

Thinking and speaking speeds

We can be forgiven for our 'ums' and 'errs' when we present, discuss or argue since some topics require considerably more mental processing, increasing the rate of conscious thought and the complexity of the cognitive (thinking) load. Obviously, a complex or a high amount of information will take extra time to process; you will need time for your speech to slow down whilst that part of the left brain works overtime on the appropriate language structure and vocabulary. Consequently, we fill the space with the 'ums' and 'errs' made possible by the time lag. It's like walking up a steep hill; because of the extra effort required our steps become slower and we begin to puff. In much the same way, with greater complexity of information our speech slows and we 'um' and 'err' for a 'breath of thinking time'.

These 'filler' words or sounds, which we all use occasionally, are useful in allowing ourselves a fraction of a second to collect our thoughts before continuing. Whilst some people can speak without putting their brains in gear, these verbal delay tactics are useful for they enable our brains to catch up to our mouths. Verbal tics are then the perfect linguistic discourse marker or stalling tactic to facilitate thinking before continuing the conversation or delivering the intended substantive response.

Like everything else with usage behaviour, this becomes a habit and a habit becomes an entrenched and intrinsic part of ourselves. Just as children by the age of about eight are fluent in two forms of English language: the first which they use with their friends in the playground, complete with those colourful words which they dare not use when they speak the other, second, variant of English at home. If eight-year-olds can master the technique, so can we. Tics can also be contagious (Peter Cook, the comedian of the 1960s, almost had the whole of Britain saying 'actually'). If you suffer from tics, ask a good friend to bring it to your attention every time you use your pet word. Thanks to the wonders of technology you can even get a wrist band which, after programming, delivers a little shock as a reminder every time you utter your personal and much-loved individual tic.

▶ brilliant example

Verbal tics do provide some clinical advantage. Not so long ago I was working with a man on a psychological problem. He had been to other psychologists and possibly came to me, as a management psychologist, as a last resort. In addition to his difficulty, this client had a severe tic, continually using the word 'basically'. During his assessment he continually made statements such as, 'Basically my problem is …', 'Basically what I try to do …', 'Basically what I want is…', 'What I enjoy basically is …', 'My wife and I basically …'.

Now I did not know what he meant by his tic but it was obviously very important to him. During his assessment and our following sessions, every now and again I popped his tic into my vocabulary as often as I could without being a mimic. He responded well and gained relief from his difficulty. Afterwards he was very flattering, complimenting me by saying, 'Basically, Max, you are the first psychologist I could understand and … well … basically … I want to thank you for being so helpful.' So, basically, Max felt very good that day!

Accents and speed of speech

For some time now outsourcing has become the flavour of the month in cost-saving drives. Contact centres, helplines, inward- and outward-bound customer service centres have been relocated to counties where pay rates are low but English, of a fashion, is spoken. This is a sensible strategy if cost saving is your main priority, but those who recommend it overlook something very important: as we have said before, like likes relating to like. You are asking for help on your computer and not only can you not understand why you have problem and how it can be solved, but you have the additional difficulty of cutting through an unfamiliar accent. It is almost as if you need a helpline to help you with your helpline.

No offence to those 'third world' (fast becoming old world) countries, but even in Britain Geordies are better at persuading, selling and helping Geordies than somebody from Tunbridge Wells; Scots do well in Scotland; and it even works in Cornwall where the differences in accent are very subtle indeed. Pronounce Tiddy Oggy inappropriately and you are definitely dead in your steak, swedes and potatoes.

Do not attempt to copy the accent of the person you are with, but there is something that you can do to facilitate rapport, persuasion and influencing, and that is to match the speed of speech captured in the accent.

In the USA, because of distance, there is much more selling done 'over the phone'. As achieving sales is critical to commercial success, much research on the effect of speed of speech has been commissioned in this area, even as long as 60 years ago. It was found that speaking at a similar speech rate to another increased your credibility and so improved your ability to influence the listener. Whilst, as we have suggested elsewhere, being enthusiastic is persuasive, where the words are spoken at a different rate to that of the listener their influence is significantly diluted.

brilliant recap

- Use the other person's preferred speech structure to aid their comprehension.
- Make allowances for the other person's disposition.
- Where appropriate, and not too often, use the person's verbal tic to aid their understanding.
- Do not attempt to copy the person's accent.
- Speak at the same pace as the other person.
- Speak at the same level of volume as the other person.

References

[1] Myers, K., Briggs, I. and Myers, P. B. (1980, 1995), *Gifts Differing: Understanding Personality Type*.

[2] *The New York Times*, transcript of the Caroline Kennedy interview with Nicholas Confessore and David M. Haibfinger, 27 December 2008.

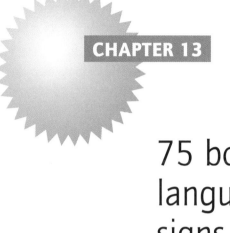

CHAPTER 13

75 body-language signs and what they might mean

Becoming bodylingual fluent

Trawling through the research for this book, one of my clients and I listed as many body-language signs as were mentioned or illustrated. Please use them for easy reference or perhaps for testing yourself on your observational skills.

However, it is very important to remember Caveat 1 on page 14. It will lead to nonsense if when observing just one body movement you interpret it as meaning something or an emotion. Seeing three swallows is a good indication the summer is on the way – three combined body movements, preferably more, should be used before you begin to make assumptions and interpretations.

The 75 body-language signs*

Physical sign	Possible meaning
1 Adam's apple bobbing	Anxiety, lying
2 Arm in front of body, touching or holding handbag, jewellery, shirt cuff, etc.	Insecurity
3 Arms and hands in the 'Adam position'	Insecurity
4 Arms and palms open	Open, honest

▶

* Based on the initial work of Gabrielle Griffin, Sydney, Australia.

Physical sign	Possible meaning
5 Arms crossed on chest	Putting a barrier between someone or something they do not accept, thus showing a negative attitude
6 Arms crossed – one holding other arm	Insecurity
7 Arms holding handbag, cup (etc.) as a barrier	Insecurity
8 Blading	Wanting to protect oneself
9 Blinking (increased)	Anxiety
10 Breathing in deeply	Relaxation, acceptance
11 Chin stroking	Making a decision, evaluating
12 Duchenne smile	Welcoming, wanting to be friends, approval
13 Eye rubbing	Confusion, tiredness
14 Eyes glaze	Disinterest, thinking
15 Face-touching, including mouth, eyes, ears, neck	Concealing the truth or nervousness
16 Fingers (or glasses, etc.) in mouth	Evaluation or needs reassurance
17 Foot pointing	Foot points in direction of attention (e.g. at the door if they want to leave, or points to someone they find attractive)
18 Foot tapping	Boredom
19 Grooming another	Desire to be intimate
20 Grooming self	Showing interest in another
21 Hand chopping	Aggressive emphasis
22 Hand gripping wrist with arms behind back	Total confidence or frustration and attempting self-control (the higher the arm grip, the higher the level of frustration or anger)
23 Hand resting against head	Interested evaluation
24 Hand slapping back of neck	Feeling threatened or angry

Physical sign	Possible meaning
25 Hands – both supporting the face, or the face rests on flat hands	A feminine action to look attractive to attract a man's attention
26 Hands clenched	Frustration (the higher the level of frustration, the higher the hands)
27 Hands – holding behind the back	Confident, authoritative
28 Hands in pockets	To look casual, to say 'Impress me', or the person does not want to participate
29 Hands on hips	Using space to show dominance
30 Hands open and palms up	Submission
31 Hands – rubbing palms together	Positive expectation
32 Hands – steepled, tips of fingers touching	Confident, relaxed, self-assured
33 Hands supporting	Expressing power through using space
34 Handshake: elbow grasp	An attempt at power, showing intimacy of friendship
35 Handshake: palm down	An attempt at power and control
36 Handshake: palm up	Giving the other person control
37 Handshake: shoulder hold	An attempt at power, shows close intimacy
38 Handshake: upper arm grip	An attempt at power
39 Handshake: vertical palms and similar pressure	Shows respect, recognises equality and encourages rapport
40 Handshake: wrist hold	Acceptable when people are close
41 Hand-to-face gestures	Negative attitude, lying or nervousness
42 Hyperventilating	Fear, anxiety
43 Leaning forward	Interest, acceptance
44 Legs crossed	Closed, submissive or defensive attitude; in women it shows comfort

Physical sign	Possible meaning
45 Legs crossed whilst sitting next to someone, with leg furthest away from other person crossed so that it is nearest that person	Acceptance of/liking the other person
46 Legs in figure-four cross – one foot resting on other knee	Confidence; dominant, competitive attitude
47 Legs open (males)	Openness or dominance
48 Legs spread (males)	Use of space to establish authority
49 Lip biting	Anxiety, holding back a comment
50 Lip licking	Anxiety, attraction
51 Looking at watch	Wish to get away, boredom, inattention
52 Mirroring	Being in rapport
53 Mouth covering	Wanting to ask a question, about to lie
54 Movement backwards	Disagreement or anxiety
55 Movement forward	Interest
56 Palm closed and pointed finger	Anger to achieve submission or agreement
57 Palm down	Projecting authority
58 Palm up	Acceptance, readiness to listen
59 Preening	Wanting to be or being attractive
60 Quick/sharp intake of breath	Surprise, shock
61 Seating position – chairs directly opposite	Competitive, defensive position
62 Seating position – chairs side-by-side on inward angles	Cooperative position
63 Smile – lower face only	Submission, insincerity
64 Smiling (full face)	Welcoming, non-threatening, asking to be accepted
65 Smirk	Arrogance, insincerity

Physical sign	Possible meaning
66 Speech – fluent and fast	Enthusiasm
67 Speech – suddenly slow	Lying
68 Standing tall	Wishing to dominate, appear attractive, in control
69 Steepling	Confidence; or – when someone is talking – means 'Impress me'
70 Teeth clenched	Frustration, anger
71 Thumb displays, often protruding from hands in jacket or trouser pockets	Superiority, dominance, striking a pose of authority
72 Thumbs tucked into belt/ pocket	Sexually aggressive attitude
73 Tic, increased use of	Anxiety
74 Touching self	Anxiety
75 Turning away	Wish to terminate the conversation

CHAPTER 14

Putting it into practice

Advice before you begin your practice

As you become more aware of body language, remember the following useful advice:

1 People who know you, whether they know it or not, have invested time and effort in understanding you as you have been and as you are now. When* you begin to develop some of the skills covered in this book your behaviour will change. Not only will this surprise other people but they will have to get to know you again, and as a result attempts will be made to keep you like your old self.

2 Up until now you have spent the whole of your life being the way you are, so even with the strongest will in the world and the strongest of motivation, your behaviour will not change overnight. Change in behaviour takes time, unless of course you allow yourself to be placed in a dark room with a dripping tap and an evil psychologist to 'look after you' for a month or so! There will be slippage back to the way you have always behaved, but remember: PPO – persistence pays off.

3 Remember what a baby does when they have just learnt to walk and wants to get from A to B quickly; they crawl because they know it is safer, faster and they feel more confident and relaxed. We are not that much different as

---

* Notice the assumptive use of 'when' here rather than 'if'.

adults; when stressed, challenged, or finding things difficult we revert or regress to the old self and discard the new because it is too hard. If you do this often enough, like New Year's resolutions made with the encouragement of beverages at Hogmanay, you soon give up.

4 Americans have a saying: 'By the inch it is a synch but by the yard it's bl★★dy hard.' This is good advice. Develop just one skill at a time. Treat these activities like a salami sausage which no one eats all at once. Develop these body language skills one at a time, slice by slice, and one day you will find it necessary to buy another length of salami!

5 Set yourself sensible targets. If a reasonably fit person went to a sports coach and said, 'I am going to run in the marathon in one month's time', the coach knows that this is over-ambitious and not possible. When the aspiring athlete fails, their ego will take such a knock that they will not try again, when if they had set themselves reasonable and achievable targets, they could certainly have completed the distance.

'If the doors of perception were cleansed everything would appear to man as it is, infinite. For man has closed himself up, till he sees all things through narrow chinks of his cavern.'

William Blake, *The Marriage of Heaven and Hell*

Blake's wise words remind us that we only see, hear, touch and smell with specialist parts of our bodies. This is how we experience our world 'through the narrow chinks' of our individual caverns. The world is far greater – in a way we see what we want to see and hear what we want to hear.

Hopefully in this introduction to body language we have mentioned some or many things that you did not appreciate before and consequently have not seen or heard – or seen and heard but have not appreciated their possible meaning. When we begin to consciously employ or orientate our five senses we see, hear and feel much more that we ever did before in similar situations. In a way we develop an understanding of body language when we are in a state of conscious incompetence. There is always a large gap between knowledge and skill.

brilliant example

Knowledge of how to ride a bike is minimal – you balance, turn the peddles and steer using the brakes as necessary. Now ask yourself, how long did it take you, in terms of practice, before you were competent?

One of the good things about the activities later in this chapter is that you can practise them in private or safe situations, gaining mastery before you need to use them. NLP suggests a helpful approach to our development of our personal skills' levels, which can be thought of as a process moving through four overlapping stages. To illustrate this, the figure on the next page uses the example of a verbal tic.

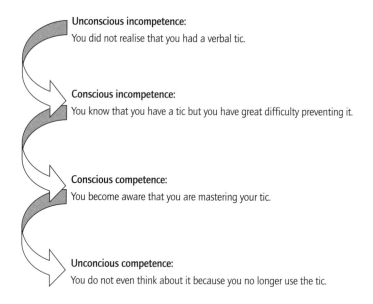

Unconscious incompetence:
You did not realise that you had a verbal tic.

Conscious incompetence:
You know that you have a tic but you have great difficulty preventing it.

Conscious competence:
You become aware that you are mastering your tic.

Unconcious competence:
You do not even think about it because you no longer use the tic.

Picture challenges

Try answering the questions posed by these pictures (possible answers on page 226).

A Too close for comfort

What are the clusters that you can see here for both the male and the female, and what are they communicating to each other? See if you can find eight signs in the cluster for each party.

B Pleased to see you

How is the female communicating that she is pleased to see the person (male) approaching from her right? She is giving eight body-language signs that she is pleased to see the person, can you identify them all?

C Stages of not coping

What is the common body language in these three pictures and what is different in each that shows a progression from pictures 1 to 3?

D Dressing up and dressing down

This executive is being interviewed for a position. Just on his clothes, why is it that the man on the right has let himself down in his dress? What are the eight possible dress errors here?

E Male sexual displays

How is this man showing off his manhood?

F Mona Lisa

What is her body language saying?

Activities to develop your skill level

1 Person perception training

Spend 30 minutes sitting in a public place and observe people from a distance – shopping malls, train stations and parks at lunchtime all provide wonderful observation opportunities. Examine body type, gait, hair style, make-up, dress, shoes, accessories, etc., and ask yourself 'What does this tell me about this person?' Sherlock Homes was great at this because, in his own words:

'When you have eliminated the impossible, whatever remains, however improbable, must be the truth.'

When I lectured at Westminster University I invited my social psychology students to carry a clipboard on the Circle line on the London Underground or somewhere similar. Their task was to observe other passengers and then, after explaining what their project was they then discussed their observations with that passenger.* For the students, following the life-learning maxim 'You get things right by getting them wrong' greatly improved their powers of observation. So often we do not follow up on the learning opportunities that life continually presents us.

'We had the experience but missed the meaning.'

T. S. Eliot, *The Four Quartets*

2 Self-instruction or affirmation

When you are on your own, instruct yourself, saying, 'I am confident', 'I communicate well', 'I am relaxed', or whatever

---

* Interestingly, when this has been done there was not one passenger who objected. However, you should initiate the conversation, explaining that you are studying body language. Until you grow in confidence, begin with people like yourself in terms of gender, age and style.

affirmation is appropriate. As strange as this might seem it does help you behave accordingly. Do this often and then, if necessary, use the same instructions to yourself in public situations. To a certain extent we are what we tell ourselves we are.

brilliant tip

To increase your personal confidence, commit to saying your affirmation with great determination just before you go to sleep and again first thing in the morning. (From Brian Lacey, American motivational speaker.)

3 Walk tall

An activity you might like to try is to spend a day walking tall, to see how it affects your self-esteem. For most people it increases their ego strength in as much as they feel good about themselves, and increases their feelings of optimism and confidence as well. High ego strength usually results in improved performance.

4 Eye contact

This is an essential skill in whatever context you want to establish a relationship. There is good advice from an excellent book by Tonya Reiman entitled *The Power of Body Language*:

'If you have trouble maintaining eye contact, you must work on this critical skill. Studies have found that employers view prospective hires who don't make eye contact as unattractive, detached, passive, incompetent and lacking composure and social skills.'

With a mirror, make eye contact with yourself and have fun staring yourself out.

Try playing the children's game 'Gunfighters and Samurai', in which you attempt to stare down a friend. The loser is the person who looks away first. Up the anti with a 'no-blink' rule; if you find yourself losing you can cheat by looking between and not into their eyes. One further tip for winners: do not move into the other person's intimate space, as the further away you are means your partner cannot tell that you're not playing fair.

Practise catching the eyes of people who 'play' a role and are not expected to interact with you, such as ticket collectors, policemen or janitors. When they catch you looking, hold their gaze and smile as you make a friendly comment on the weather or something equally bland. Do this with and without a smile and see what happens.

Once you have mastered this, then for the advance diploma catch the eye of a fellow lift passenger, smile, and make a suitable comment. It is best to start with people your own age and gender preference so that there are no 'cross' or misunderstood communications!

Health note: Do not play stare down with dogs you do not know unless you are wearing armour!

5 Smile

When in a public place and someone catches your eye (when they are looking at you and not vice versa) give a genuine smile whilst dipping your head (the latter to show you mean no harm) and see how many people return your smile. Smile at people who are not of the same skin tone as yourself and see what happens.

Serious warning: Do not try this in public toilets or similar – you do not want to be accused of soliciting.

If you are very shy and find smiling at strangers too challenging, then work up to it by going to a large supermarket and smiling at mothers with small children under two – this is socially acceptable as every mother wants her beautiful baby to be pleasing to others.

6 Pupils

Make a collection of pictures, e.g. houses, clothes, animals, etc., – about ten should do – each with a number. Then sit opposite a friend and watch the pupils of their eyes as you show the pictures one at a time. As you do this, develop a benchmark by asking yourself 'What is their average pupil size?'

Do not write notes because in doing so you might influence your 'subject', contaminate your data and not achieve the results you want.

When you show your battery of pictures for the second time, watch to see if there is any significant increase in pupil size for a particular picture or pictures.

Record and remember those pictures where your friend's pupils dilate. If you are not sure, repeat the process slowly.

Once you are confident about which pictures are significant for your friend, record that fact, without your friend seeing, and place your record face down near your friend.

Then invite your friend to pick out their top three most interesting, attractive, appealing – whatever category is appropriate – pictures to them.

Then hopefully, as if by magic, your lists should be similar.

7 Hands

If you are one of those people who wave their arms about beyond shoulder width or above your neck it could be interpreted as a limitation on your fluency, your level of confidence, or that you are not used to speaking in public and you feel you need to be charismatic to maintain your listener's attention.

Spend time speaking with your fingers interlocked in a steeple position whilst sitting, or if standing put your hands by your side – if you are a chronic waver put your hand behind your back. All these positions will make you aware that you have a strong tendency to speak in your own personal version of semaphore. Being conscious of your 'flagging' is the largest part of curing the habit.

If your arms are independent of your torso and you are an incurable waver, then only let your arms loose and do their thing when you want to emphasise what you are saying, so that these expressive limbs are in sync with what you are saying.

8 Speech (theirs)

Listen for verbal tics (we all have them) and sprinkle them into your speech and listen to the result.

When talking to strangers note their speed of speech and match it in your conversation with them.

Unless you are very gifted, do not attempt to mimic the accent of the other person. They have spent all their life speaking the way they do and can spot a fake a mile off.

9 Speech (yours)

With a voice recorder:

1 Practise changing the speed of your speech.

2 Practise varying the pitch of your voice.

3 Practise the same speech in your normal voice and then 'through' a smile.

4 Practise the same speech sitting down and standing up.

5 Practise the same speech several times, placing the emphasis on different words each time.

6 Practise saying, 'They are eating apples' and 'The killing of the hunters was terrible' so that you achieve two different meanings for each.

7 Practise reading the telephone directory with enthusiasm and emphasis, first placing the emphasis on the name, next reading the address, and finally reading the telephone number.

With this last activity put into practice the words of John Wesley:

'Catch on fire with enthusiasm and people will come from miles to watch you burn.'

When you play the voice recorder back, listen to yourself and, possibly with a friend, discuss the differences and then answer the questions: 'What works for me? What do I want to use in the future?' Then you have to practise, practise until it becomes natural for you – just as some male pop stars sing falsetto, which is not natural, but with practice they can do it without thinking or straining their voices.

10 Personal space

When in social gatherings, observe the distance people maintain between each other. When talking to someone consciously, move very slightly towards or away from them and observe what happens.

Personal space is culturally determined and can lead to the 'cocktail dance', when there is, for example, a diplomatic meeting with people from different countries. In their attempt to converse with each other using their own culturally determined personal space, as they move forward (Asian and Arab people) others move back (English and East-coast Americans).

11 Dress and first impressions

Think about the way you dress. Are you a 'dedicated follower of fashion'? What or who has influenced you? What statements are you making or how might people stereotype you by what you wear?

Dress formally and ask strangers the way to somewhere; dress informally with untidy hair and dirty hands and shoes and ask the same sort of person the exact same question in exactly the same place as you were in the first situation. Then reflect on the responses that you received in the two different situations.

Observe how the senior managers in your organisation or industry dress and how you dress for work. Is there a difference and should you do anything about it?

Sit in a public place – train stations are great for this – and 'people watch'; consider especially their clothes and from the detail attempt to guess their occupations. Even if you get it wrong you will learn about your own stereotypes and prejudices.

Look at professional magazines. Look at the photographs in the magazine of your profession or your industry and ask yourself 'What image are they trying to project and why?' and 'Do I need to do this?'

Look at my photo in my bio at the front of the book.

- What am I trying to say to you about myself?
- What three adjectives am I attempting to promote about myself?
- What did you pick on to support your view?
- What did I get right or wrong? Why?

12 Spotting tells

This is fun. Ask a friend to hide a coin in one of their hands then put both hands behind their back. Their hands are then brought forward and you have to guess which hand has the coin.

Look at your friend's hands (one may be higher than the other or there is some incongruity about them), prominent eye direction, nose pointing and/or body lean. One or several observations in combination will indicate which hand has the coin. After three goes you should be able to spot the individual 'tell' of your friend. Test it on the fourth go; if you get it right tell your friend that now you have stopped playing and will be serious for the next six goes. Magic! And good practice too!

13 Proxemics magic

You will need:

- Space of at least 4 metres.
- Two chairs which you can move easily.
- Pencil and paper.

Say to a person that you have been observing them and you would like to see if you are right in your analysis. Do not mention personal zones or body language, as some people will deliberately not play the game.

In your friend's presence, but without letting them see you, draw a straight line with a break in the middle. Fold it and set it aside. Get two chairs and place them 3 metres apart, then each of you should sit down facing each other. Invite your friend to move their chair towards you because you are going to have a conversation about holidays. As they move towards you do not let them move their chair or their body to the side but come to you 'head on'. Do not let them cross their legs. Once they have come close enough, ask them if they feel comfortable. As soon as they say 'Yes' say, 'Do not move' (as some people as soon as they stop move their shoulders back to rest on the chair) then say, 'Without moving your shoulders I want you to raise your left arm straight in front of you'. You do the same, but with your right arm, so that now both arms are parallel to the ground and pointing at each other. With your friend, note the distance between your middle fingers. Put your arms down, fetch the paper and put it on your lap, then wave your hand over the folded paper saying, in a deep and mysterious voice, 'Proxemics, proxemics'. Open the paper and show it to your friend; the distance you have drawn should be almost exactly the same as you achieved in the game.

If they are impressed and want to know more about body language do not lend them your book – ask them to buy it! Thank you!

The distances of the break in the line you draw are:

- Male to male   = 2cm break.
- Female to male   = 3cm break.
- Female to female   = 2.5cm break.

For obvious reasons this will not work with family members or those with whom you have been intimate. Also, your friend has to have enjoyed the same cultural upbringing as yourself.

14 Assertiveness

For students at the University of Westminster covering various aspects of social psychology, as part of their training they were sent out on to the Circle line of the London Underground just before rush hour. Their role was to go to a person sitting down and say 'Excuse me, but can I sit down please?' This could be varied in many ways, including: saying the assumptive 'thank you' rather than please; speaking softly and loudly, with or without a smile; moving in and out of the seated individual's personal space; dressing formally and informally; asking men and asking women; asking someone young and someone middle aged (older, handicapped people and pregnant women were not to be asked). Should there be compliance or a refusal the person was told (very quickly, if there was any indication of aggression) why they had been asked. Then the following week we would discuss the results. The students were amazed that in all the different conditions most of the people they asked complied immediately with no challenge whatsoever.

This is the most challenging of all these activities and I suggest you do it with a friend nearby to give you confidence.

15 Mirroring

When you are in rapport with another person it is very natural to move in the same way as they do. From a discrete distance, observe people chatting to each other and you will very quickly notice that as one of the participants moves, soon the other person will move in the same way. Their arms will move at the same time, they will move forward and back at the same time, and if drinking they will sup at the same time. What is fascinating is that they will be undertaking this social dance without even knowing it.

Sit opposite a friend. In silence they should move their hands and bodies slowly and your role is to mirror their movements in the smoothest way possible. You take turns at this. After two or three goes you should be able to anticipate your friend's movements and consequently your moves should become increasingly smoother.

Next, ask your friend to chat about their last holiday, or any subject they have a keen interest in, while you keep your body still. Then ask your friend which part they enjoyed most, or what did they found interesting (or a similar question to encourage some enthusiasm in your friend), and gradually begin to mirror them. Keep asking questions to keep the conversation going. On conclusion of the conversation, ask your friend if they noticed your mirroring and when it started. If they say 'Yes' and provide specifics, were there any movements that they missed? If they perceived most of them, keep practising!

Advice

Do not consciously mirror people socially; if you are thinking too much about what you are doing you need more practice with friends. It is best to get to almost 'unconscious competence' before you let yourself loose on an inspecting public.

To practise on your own, turn off the TV during a chat show and mirror the host or their guests as they speak.

What is important here for body language is that when you are conscious of the other person's body language, if you are in rapport with them, then they might be changing their movements just because you have. This is a contamination spiral; you are watching a mirror image of yourself and without knowing it you are contaminating the situation. In other words, who is mirroring who?

16 Observation

Most people when they are alone in a diner, waiting room or pub start playing with their mobile phone. Why not hone your body language skills instead, just watching individuals, couples and groups? Your experience will naturally kick in – we can't help but make judgements about people (see Solomon's 7/11 phenomena on page 36), but now ask yourself what you are picking up on. How are you justifying your initial conclusions about the individual(s), their relationships to each other and their emotions? Are you picking up on the same thing most of the time – if so, does this indicate bias on your part, so should you broaden your observation techniques?

Advice

Please plan and undertake your observation missions cautiously and from a sensible distance – you don't want to be accused of and personally challenged for being a voyeur, otherwise you will have to immediately and rapidly put into practice all your submissive body skills!

A further observation

It is often said that television has destroyed the art of conversation. In fact, it is not the TV per se but how the TV dominates and influences the seating arrangement in a home. It is difficult to enjoy a conversation when you have to turn your head to the side to talk to a companion, even if they are sitting comfortably. So the location of domestic conversations have moved from the living room to the kitchen.

Have you ever thought why it is that in the city, where it is crowded on the pavement with lots of people all going their separate ways, you rarely make any psychological connection, yet if you just met one of those people coming towards you on a country lane you would probably initiate or respond to a friendly salutation such as 'Hello' or 'Good afternoon'?

brilliant example

Being an Australian I just love the scene in the Australian film of 1986 when Crocodile Dundee is taking his first trip in a New York cab. The cab stops at a traffic light. Dundee, coming from country Australia, winds down the window, grabs the nearest pedestrian's hand and says 'G'day'. To see the non-verbal response of the New Yorker is classic and can be very easily understood in any culture.

Note: All of the activities here are suggestions only and not instructions. The author and publisher cannot be held liable should the outcome of an activity suggested be unacceptable in any way.

Conclusion

Ethics, body language and manipulation

Ab imo pectore

This book is essentially about effecting and understanding our relations with others and ourselves. As we act and behave we have choices that do have consequences for ourselves and others. Ethical decisions are founded on values such as mutual respect, trust and responsibility, which we have irrespective of our spiritual or cultural homes. Acting ethically does not come without a price, because we live in a world of limited resources even in the area of family, children, friends and all other interpersonal relations. In the end each one of us has to decide whether or not what we want from others diminishes who we are or want to be as a person. I write this section because as a psychologist and as an Anglican priest I would be ashamed if anyone used this little work to manipulate another person for their own benefit.

An understanding of body language – although much of it we know intuitively – helps us to communicate and understand others more accurately, and perhaps they us. Throughout the book we have spoken about how to get into rapport more easily, how to persuade others, how to make ourselves more attractive and how to act when we wish to be attractive to others. In all of this we are trying 'to create the outcome that we wish', otherwise why would we do it?

Are we being honest?

'This above all: to thine own self be true, and it must follow, as the night the day, thou canst not be false to any man.'

William Shakespeare, *Hamlet*, Act I, Scene III

What I think Polonius is really saying to his son Laertes here is that sometimes we spend too much time on who we want to be and not nearly enough on who we really are.

We all know that if we are pleased with our physical appearance, or not so pleased, we can either congratulate or commiserate that we recruited the right or the wrong grandparents. This we know; at a mature age my hairstyle is exactly the same as that of my father and my grandfathers; my height and body shape come from the same mould.

What is now coming to light is that our genes, much more than our environment and upbringing, account for significant dispositional traits (how happy, anxious, stressed and assertive, etc. we are) than was previously thought. In a sense we are what we are because of our DNA – and we behave accordingly, thus manifesting the matching body language.

The evidence is overwhelming that those with open personalities, who enjoy a positive self-concept will be more successful – in a worldly sense. But what about those who were not blessed with innate self-confidence and tend be more interpersonally quiet? Generally they are hesitant and slow of speech because they like to observe and reflect before they open their mouths. They are happy inside their heads, naturally not gregarious, and their eye contact with others is usually less. Confident but high introverts can sometimes fit into this category.

The message here, then, for those of us who would wish to change is we have to be 'contingent'. Being contingent means telling ourselves that in certain situations it would be more appropriate to alter our normal behaviour, thereby responding in a way called for by the situation. As a simple example: most parents spoil their children but on occasion they have to be strict and say something like 'You must not swear' because of the circumstances (then giggle about the child's new vocabulary in private). It is the same for us if we are normally shy: this is healthy, but on occasions it will be necessary for us to come out of our shells and be assertive or appear more confident than we really are. This requires a different set of body language skills, but we do this consciously. In this way we are being true to ourselves yet behaving in a contingent way, justified by the particular circumstances – utilitarianism with a slight difference (which we shall come to later).

So whether it is important to get into rapport with someone (such as in a networking situation), appear more confident, be assertive, pass an interview, or find a new partner, developing our body-language skills will be inordinately useful.

Commonsense and experience tell us that not all the strategies and techniques suggested here will work all the time, with all the people, in all situations. If they did, the modest investment you made in purchasing this short volume could be increased ten fold.

When we wish to understand and use our understanding of body language and non-verbal behaviour it does not automatically suggest that we wish to manipulate others. However, with a little thought and reflection you can see how such an unfortunate occasion could occur. As humans we not only arrive out of the womb screaming, but also from that point on we are masters of manipulation. In fact, up until the age of about two we are at our most influential, exerting great power over adults. Babies naturally follow one of the most powerful rules of persuasion, which simply states:

'If what you are doing does not work, try something else.'

When small, all babies' needs are legitimate and one could say natural and normal. Consequently it would be inappropriate to use the word 'manipulation' in this context. The baby's legitimate behaviour is to influence the parents. So indeed it is natural for us, as more mature humans, to want to create for ourselves 'outcomes that we wish'. However, when we refer to the thesaurus for the word 'influence', we find synonyms such as 'pressure', 'persuade' and 'manipulate'.

Perhaps, since we all want to create outcomes that suit us, when thinking about our own and the behaviour of others it would be possible to use this concept of achieving what you wish by declining the verb like so:

I sway people to   *(I certainly never manipulate people)*
achieve an outcome

You persuade people to   *(You sometimes manipulate people)*
achieve an outcome

They manipulate people to   *(They manipulate people all the time)*
achieve an outcome

Consequentialism, categorical imperatives and utilitarianism

A moment's reflection will tell us that we tend only to be concerned with the ethics of interpersonal behaviour if someone uses us to 'create an outcome that they want' and we become damaged in some way socially, financially or personally. Words like unfair, not right, self-centred and inequitable immediately spring to mind. No one likes unknowingly to be used by another, but ... but what we are unlikely to do is, when we act with the best intentions and feel good about ourselves we hardly ever spend a moment to consider how our actions were received. Was the outcome good or bad, negative or positive? If it was negative, inappropriate, or hurtful, are we entitled to justify our use of body language and non-verbal behaviour skills by saying 'Well, I meant well'? The quote 'The road to hell is paved with good intentions' captures this concept with a succinct beauty and brevity. So even with the best of intentions, when we apply these skills without reflection on the outcome for the other individual, it can have unethical and have unforseen conclusions, even if we really meant well.

If we only thought of the outcomes rather than the intentions when considering the ethics here then we could fall into the abyss of consequentialism. Kant's categorical imperatives do not help us here very much either, nor does the utilitarianism of Hobbes (which at its barest weighs benefits and harms, and concludes that the 'right' action is the one that produces maximum good for the most people with no consideration as to whether that good is produced by manipulation or lies, which can be easy with the skilled use of body language). This is rather like America and Israel's response to terrorism – a pre-emptive strike is permissible because the consequences of not acting could be far worse.

Quo vadis? Aristotle's Nicomachean ethics, better known today as 'virtue ethics', to my mind, comes to the rescue, suggesting that we can achieve good things by being good ourselves, and although very testing such behaviour is possible to develop.[1] Put in another way, we can employ the golden rule, sometimes referred to as 'reciprocity ethics':

'*Do unto others as you would have them do unto you.*'

Millions of people spend much of their lives attempting to achieve this maxim when they wish to be more effective in their personal relations. In economic terms this demand is 'inelastic'* in as much as whatever you do it is not enough.

---

* Desire for something that does not vary despite increases or decreases in price.

At an intuitive level, when we use some of the skills suggested here, only we know whether our intention is to sway, to influence or to manipulate another. It is not so much our logic, we just know because we are challenged by our own moral code and values. So, to be ethical in our interpersonal behaviour is first to be aware of our intentions but also to employ the same moral imperative to review outcomes and learn from them. In the wise words of Oscar Wilde:

'Every great mistake has a halfway moment, a split second when it can be recalled and perhaps remedied.'

The Picture of Dorian Gray (1891)

So, perhaps as you enter your social world armed with the skills of body language and the understanding of non-verbal communication, hopefully expanded by the contents of this book, my sincerest request as a psychologist and as an Anglican priest is that in all our interpersonal relations (yes, that includes me as well) we act with the very best of intentions – but above all we should do no harm.

Vincit qui se vincit.

Be brilliant!

Reference

[1] Hackman, M. Z. and Johnson, C. E. (1996), *Leadership: A Communication Perspective.*

Appendix 1

Possible answers to questions raised in the book

Answers to the picture on page 5

The emotion here is anger, shown by:

1 Brows are furrowed.

2 A forward lean – to get into the personal space of the other person.

3 Nose flare.

4 Chin jutting.

5 Clenched fist – being ready to strike.

6 Eyes totally focused and wide to see as much as possible.

7 Finger pointing in combination with a half-fist.

Answers to the crossed arms challenge on page 15:

1 They may be cold.

2 They feel comfortable that way.

3 They like to hug themselves.

4 The chair has no arm to rest on.

5 They have a tummy ache.

6 They are embarrassed about the size of their breasts or man boobs.

7 This is the correct way to pay attention (especially children).

8 They have an itch in their armpit.

9 They want to hide their paunch.

10 They want to show that they have just got engaged.

11 They want to show off their tan/slender arms/biceps.

12 They have a cracked rib and want to keep very still.

13 They want to show off their expensive watch.

14 They want you to impress them.

15 They might be of the opinion this is the correct way to sit at a presentation.

16 They are anxious and need to self-touch.

17 They are sitting the way their parent(s) always used to sit.

18 They are sitting the way their parent(s) told them to sit.

19 They have a button missing from their blouse/shirt.

20 They spilt their lunch-time Bolognese on their blouse/shirt.

Answers to the personal zone picture on page 31

1 Whilst she is still smiling it is only a half smile.

2 Her shoulders have turned away slightly.

3 Her body has turned away more than her shoulders.

4 Her feet are indicating a wish to move away.

Answers to the mirroring picture on page 88

The cluster for mirroring is:

1 Leaning towards each other.

2 Both sets of arms are in the same position.

3 Both are steepling.

4 Both are smiling.

5 Both have a head tilt.

Possible next moves are:

The male: Turns his head to look at the female, thus being
             in sync, or turns his body to the left to show total
             interest in her.

The female: Reaches for the glass, moving her hand forward
             like his and moving into intimate space. She might
             even stroke the glass as it would be too 'forward' to
             stroke him.

Answers to the posture picture on page 139

Male posture:

● Attempting maximum eye contact: to encourage familiarity/
  intimacy.

● Standing tall: to look impressive and confident.

● Standing 'square on': showing that he finds the woman
  attractive and to display as much of himself as possible, as
  well as showing confidence and friendship.

- Standing almost in the woman's personal zone: indicating a desire to be friends.
- Left arm on chair: to appear casual.
- Right arm akimbo: to maximise his size.
- Both arm positions: to block other males approaching.

Female posture:

- Lack of full smile: confirming minimal interest.
- Chin not raised: not wishing to expose or lift her bust.
- Left shoulder turning away: showing desire to break contact.
- Forearms across the body: showing a defensive position.
- Legs, especially the left, pointing away from the man: indicating a strong desire to move away.
- Feet flat on the ground: not wishing to show off her bust.

Appendix 2

Possible answers to the picture challenges on pages 199–202

A Too close for comfort

The male wants to show that he is attracted to the female by:

1 Moving into her personal space – he is on the edge of his half of the sofa.

2 Leaning towards her with his trunk.

3 Although sitting, he is attempting to square his shoulders towards her.

4 He is attempting to achieve high eye contact.

5 His elbows are splayed to make him look bigger.

6 His right arm is moving towards her.

7 His right knee is moving towards her.

8 His hands are steepled, showing confidence.

The female wants to show that she is finding his advances uncomfortable by:

1   Moving away – she is as close to the arm of the sofa as possible.

2   She is turning her head away, making her look out of the corner of her eyes.

3   Her back is straight and in no way making a physical concession to the male.

4   Her elbows are close to her sides to protect her body and hide her bust.

5   Her left forearm is extended to cover her thigh.

6   Her left shoulder is giving the cold shoulder (without being rude).

7   Her legs are crossed which is, in this situation, a defensive movement.

8   Her left leg is crossed away from the male to create additional distance.

B Pleased to see you

She is pleased because:

1   She is turning her body towards the person.

2   Her head is tilted back, revealing her throat.

3   She has a full smile with both mouth and eyes.

4   She is making eye contact.

5   Her right arm is moved back and is not defensive.

6   Her right arm is moved back to show off her bust.

7   Although her left leg is pointing away it is slightly lifted, showing the outline of her thigh.

8   The shoe of her right heel is dangling off her foot.

C The stages of not coping

What is common?

1   All are looking down.

2   All eyebrows are pressed together.

3   All have hands-to-face gestures.

What is different?

Picture 1 – Shows puzzlement, through a furrowed brow.

Picture 2 – Shows resignation, through tiredness and inactivity.

Picture 3 – Shows collapse, by shutting herself off from the world.

D Dressing up and dressing down

The man on the right has made the following mistakes for a senior exeuctive position because:

1   His tie does not match his suit.

2   The tie is not a full Windsor and not a hand in four (the schoolboy knot).

3   His top pocket has a cheap pen.

4   His watch could either be a cheap one and/or the strap should be black.

5   His shirt cuffs cannot be seen.

6   He is not wearing a black belt.

7   His socks clash with the suit.

8   His shoes should be black.

E Male sexual displays

1   His stubble is a secondary sexual indicator, suggesting virility.

2   His arms behind his head make him look larger.

3   His arms behind his head make him look confident.

4   His shirt undone is a state of undress and shows his chest.

5   Leaning back forces his crutch to be raised.

F Mona Lisa

Is she:

1   Content?

2   At peace?

3   Relaxed?

4   Bemused?

5   Confident?

6   Waiting?

7   Preoccupied?

8   Satisfied?

9   Secure in herself?

10 Day dreaming?

11 Contemplating?

12 Showing pity?

13 Bored, but too polite to show it?

14 Interested in you?

No one knows for sure – one of the mysteries of the world!

Remember: with body language there are very few absolutes, just possibilities.

Index